John's Thought and Theology
An Introduction

by

Daniel J. Harrington, S.J.

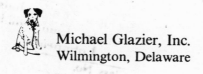

Michael Glazier, Inc.
Wilmington, Delaware

About the Author

Daniel J. Harrington, S.J., is professor of New Testament at Weston School of Theology in Cambridge, Massachusetts, and general editor of *New Testament Abstracts*. He earned his Ph.D. in Near Eastern Languages and Literatures at Harvard University in 1970. He has written regularly for the leading scholarly journals; and among his books published by Michael Glazier, Inc. are *Interpreting the New Testament: A Practical Guide; Interpreting the Old Testament: A Practical Guide; Light of All Nations: Studies on the Church in New Testament Research; The New Testament: A Bibliography; The Maccabean Revolt: Anatomy of a Biblical Revolution;* and he is editorial consultant and participant in the translation and annotation of *The Aramaic Bible (The Targums).*

First published in 1990 by Michael Glazier, Inc., 1935 West Fourth Street, Wilmington, Delaware 19805.

Library of Congress Cataloging-in-Publication Data

Harrington, Daniel J.
   John's Gospel: a guide to its thought and theology/by Daniel Harrington.
     p. cm.
    ISBN 0-89453-796-2
    1. Bible. N.T. John—Commentaries. I. Title.
    BS2615.3.H37   1990
    226.5'07—dc20   90-30920
                                         CIP

Typography by Brenda Belizzone & Mary Brown
Printed in the United States of America by St. Mary's Press.

GOOD NEWS STUDIES

Consulting Editor: Robert J. Karris, O.F.M.

Volume 33

TABLE OF CONTENTS

To Reverend John J. Collins, S.J.
On His Ninetieth Birthday
(see John 1:6-8)

Background Information

Reading John's Gospel

Many Bible readers find John's Gospel difficult. At first sight the words seem easy enough. But soon one realizes that terms like "light," "life," "world," and "Jews" are not so simple after all. And the argument is often hard to follow. The beautiful phrases and sentences often appear to float like puffy clouds across the page. But where they fit and what logic they follow are not so easy to see.

This guide to John's Gospel is meant for those who want to understand its vocabulary and logic, and so to enter the world of the Johannine community and Johannine theology. It is a "scholarly" book only in the sense that it presents the results of reading thousands of books and articles on John's Gospel by leading scholars. I try to state the results of scholarship in such a way that non-specialists can see what Johannine scholars do and perhaps themselves move into the more technical presentations listed in the bibliography. The exposition of the text is preceded by an introduction that uses three series of seven adjectives each to characterize John's Gospel.

Literary Features

• *biographical:* John tells the story of Jesus' public ministry: how he gathered disciples, performed "signs" and taught, instructed his disciples, was put to death, and appeared to his disciples. Although the Gospel may not conform to a twentieth-century definition of a biography, it does measure up to the more flexible standards of ancient biography in which the person's significance as an example (good or bad) was central. However, the claim that Jesus as God's Son revealed God, surpassed what other ancient authors said about their heroes.

• *purposeful:* Toward the end of the Gospel, the Evangelist states his reason for writing his story of Jesus: "that you may [come to] believe that Jesus is the Messiah, the Son of God, and that through this belief you may have life in his name" (20:31). There is some ambiguity in the verb "believe" that leaves unclear whether the Gospel was intended to deepen the faith of those who already believed or to attract those who had not yet believed. The consequence of belief in Jesus as Messiah and Son of God is the beginning of eternal life.

• *dramatic:* John's story of Jesus is highly dramatic. His portrait of Jesus makes his hero an attractive character, all the more so as he is played off against his disciples and opponents. The Gospel as a whole has a certain tragic movement as Jesus approaches death. The individual episodes mix narrative, dialogue, and discourse to achieve a literary variety. Jesus always expresses himself in an elevated way as befits God's Son. He enters into debate and conflict with the "Jews." Their misunderstandings allow him to explain and clarify. At the end of each episode, Jesus emerges as noble and wise.

• *sophisticated:* In the service of his dramatic program, the Evangelist uses various literary devices: misunderstanding (where the audience misses Jesus' point), double meaning (plays on words that can mean two things; "again" and "from above" in 3:1-15), irony (where the reader grasps the true meaning that eludes the speaker; see 11:50), chiasm (parallel ideas or terms pivoting around a central notion), symbolic language ("Lamb of God"), and inclusion (beginning and ending in the same way as in 1:1 and 20:28 where Jesus is called "God").

• *disjointed:* For all the dramatic skill shown in the Gospel, there are some peculiar literary inconsistencies. At the end of chapter 5 Jesus is in Jerusalem, whereas at the beginning of chapter 6 he seems to be in Galilee. After hiding from the crowds in 12:36, Jesus speaks publicly in 12:44. At the end of chapter 14, he commands the disciples, "Get up, let us go"

(14:31) but stays around for three more chapters of farewells until 18:1. Much in 13:31-14:31 is duplicated in 16:4-33. The Gospel seems to end at 20:30-31, only to start up again in chapter 21 and reach a second conclusion at 21:25.

• *traditional:* One way of accounting for the occasional literary unevenness is to assume that the Evangelist has incorporated sources into his Gospel. The prologue (1:1-18) contains fragments of an early Christian hymn. The seven major "signs" or miracle stories (2:1-12; 4:46-54; 5:1-9; 6:1-15; 6:16-21; 9:1-7; 11:1-44) were probably taken from an earlier collection. The speeches, especially the farewell discourses in chapters 13-17, may have been in circulation before the Gospel was composed. The passion narrative, though similar at some points to the other Gospels, appears to have been at one time an independent narrative, at least in part. These traditional sources at the Evangelist's disposal developed in the so-called Johannine school, which explains their literary similarities and differences.

• *different:* The Synoptic Gospels (Matthew, Mark, Luke) provide a "common view" (synopsis). But John's perspective is different. Apart from the passion narrative, almost everything in John is missing from the Synoptics, and vice versa. Much of Jesus' public ministry takes place in Jerusalem and Judea. Jesus' career spans three Passover celebrations (see 2:13; 6:4; 11:55). Nicodemus, the Samaritan woman, the man born blind, Lazarus, Philip, the beloved disciple, and Thomas are major characters. The focus of Jesus' preaching is his task of revealing his heavenly Father and his identity as the revealer. The kingdom of God is in the background. Jesus' status as preexistent Son of God, as "I AM," as "God" goes far beyond what is said about him in the other Gospels. Jesus (rather than the Jewish Law) is the definitive expression of God's will for his people.

Historical Features

• *accurate:* Where John differs from the other Evangelists on certain historical matters, it is likely that John is correct.

Jesus' public ministry probably lasted three years rather than one year. Jesus probably did visit Jerusalem more than once. Jesus probably was crucified before Passover began, not on the first day of Passover. The geographical references throughout the Gospel are accurate and suggest a first-hand acquaintance with these places in the land of Israel.

• *Jewish:* Johannine Christianity began as a movement within Judaism and faced its most severe crisis when its adherents were being expelled from the Jewish synagogues in the late first-century (see 9:22; 12:42; 16:2). From chapter 5 on, John's Gospel traces Jesus' activities by reference to the major feasts in the Jewish calendar. How Jesus fulfilled the Jewish Scriptures is a major concern throughout the Gospel. There is no doubt that Jesus and his followers are Jews. The Gospel is written in a Semitic style of Greek. As the discovery of the Dead Sea scrolls proved, the vocabulary and style are not at all foreign to Palestine in the first century. Pagan observers would have perceived the Johannine Christians to be a movement within Judaism. The Johannine Christians probably viewed themselves as practicing a more perfect form of Judaism than their rivals and ancestors did.

• *traditional:* Though put in final form in the late first century (about A.D. 90), John's Gospel at several points appeals to the testimony of one who was close to the earthly Jesus. This figure is called the "one whom Jesus loved" (13:23; 19:26; 20:2; 21:7). Someone called "the other (or another) disciple" is also mentioned in 18:15 and 20:2 (where he is identified as the "beloved disciple"). The reference to the "two disciples" (1:37) suggests that he may have been first a follower of John the Baptist. In Christian tradition this figure has been identified as John, son of Zebedee, though there are problems with that identification. The important thing is that the Johannine school traced its tradition back to the circle of Jesus' disciples and gave special attention to the "beloved disciple."

• *communal:* John's Gospel cannot be taken simply as the eyewitness report of the "beloved disciple." Rather it is the product of long reflection on Jesus that was carried on in the

Johannine community for over fifty years. The one known as the "beloved disciple" may have been the founder of this "school" or community made up largely of Jewish Christians. After the destruction of the Jerusalem temple in A.D. 70, all Jews (including Christian Jews) were forced to redefine their Judaism. In this crisis the exalted claims of the Johannine community about Jesus led to their expulsion from the synagogues and a strained relationship with other Jews. In the late first century the Gospel as we have it took shape, the literary expression of the activity of the Johannine school. It served as both a statement of the community's beliefs about Jesus and a defense against the criticisms made by outsiders. Further developments in the life of the Johannine community can be traced with the help of the Johannine epistles (1-3 John).

- *multi-leveled:* Given the long and complex development of John's Gospel, it is possible and necessary to read it at several different levels. It presents itself first and foremost as the story of Jesus' public ministry and death in the early first century (A.D. 27-30). But it uses the stories about Jesus to cast light on the crises faced by the Johannine community in its history, especially as it separated from the synagogues. Those stories were expanded and adapted over the years to provide advice for new situations, just as they have been used in church life through the centuries.

- *polemical:* The chief opponents of Jesus and his followers are the "Jews." They appear usually in negative contexts—as Jesus' opponents in debate, as his persecutors, and as the ones who convince Pontius Pilate to have Jesus executed. Since Jesus and John and the other early Christians were Jews, these "Jews" did not represent all Israel but rather a group within Israel. The negative portrayal of the "Jews" is best explained by reference to the two major levels at which the Gospel must be read. There seems to be an equation or identification between the opponents of Jesus in the early first century and the opponents of the Johannine community in the late first century. The so-called anti-Jewish elements reflect a situation in which Johannine Christians were being excluded from the synagogues and were engaged in a struggle against the "Jews" who dominated those synagogues and were contesting the Christian claim to be the people of God.

• *universal:* John's Gospel was put in final form in the late first century by a Jewish-Christian writer for a community in Palestine, Syria, or perhaps Transjordan. This community had recently been forced out or severed its ties with the local synagogue. Yet the language and ideas in John's Gospel could be understood (and still are) by people of many cultures. There is much in the Gospel that would have appealed to different currents within Judaism: wisdom, apocalyptic, sectarian, and so forth. Both Jews and non-Jews influenced by Hellenism would have found much that fascinated them. The first commentator on the Gospel was a gnostic named Heracleon, in the mid-second century. Other gnostics eagerly made use of John's Gospel in their struggles with orthodox Christians. Indeed some "gnostic" ideas may have influenced the Johannine school. Today John's Gospel exercises a particular attraction among Christians and non-Christians in India. New Christians in many lands find it their entry into the Scriptures.

Theological Features

• *christocentric:* The basic theological message of John's Gospel is simple: Jesus, the Son of God, reveals the Father. The center of the Gospel is the person and mission of Jesus. He is the "man from heaven" sent by the Father. His death was not a defeat. Rather it was the "hour" of glory in which he began his return to the Father. He invites his followers to share in his relationship with the Father—one characterized by knowledge, love, unity, and mission. In his physical absence, the Spirit-Paraclete guides and animates the community of Jesus' followers until "the last day."

• *dualistic:* As the Dead Sea scrolls and other Jewish texts have shown, many Jews in the first century, while acknowledging the supreme authority of God, divided all present reality into two camps. The children of light do the deeds of light under the leadership of the Angel of Light, and the children of darkness do the deeds of darkness under the leadership of the Angel of Darkness. This Jewish form of modified dualism found its way into early Christianity and received its strongest expression in John's Gospel. There are no "grays" in dualistic thinking. This kind of dualistic thinking is at the root of the many negative comments in John's Gospel about the "world" and the "Jews." See John 3:1-21 for a good example of Johannine dualism.

• *provocative:* Everything in John's Gospel challenges the reader to come to a decision about Jesus: What do you think of him? Are you on his side or not? What are you going to do about it? Often, by what it does not say, John's Gospel also raises questions about important aspects of Christian life and theology. Since it says nothing about Jesus' Last Supper (see Mark 14:22-25), what was the attitude of the Johannine community toward sacraments? What kind of church structures and offices did it have, since there are no hints about these in the Gospel? Since so much emphasis is placed on eternal life having already begun in the present, what is to be expected on "the last day?"

• *influential:* The Johannine presentation of Jesus, especially as this is summarized in the prologue (1:1-18), has provided the terminology and ideas for Christian theologians throughout the centuries. The doctrinal influence of John's Gospel is especially apparent in the patristic period when the early church councils made definitions about the person of Jesus. That he was divine and thus on a level with the Father and the Spirit was based on John 1:1 and 20:28. That he had both a human and a divine nature was rooted in John 1:14 ("the Word became flesh"). The pre-existence of Jesus is stated in John 1:1-2.

• *dangerous:* For all its beauty and nobility, it is possible to misuse John's Gospel. Sectarians and fundamentalists seize upon its dualism to separate from others and to deny any validity to different religious approaches. Anti-Semites exploit the negative comments about the "Jews" and apply them to all the Jewish people throughout history and today. Modern gnostics (the "New Age" movement, for example) claim John for themselves, when in fact the Johannine community opposed such thinking by insisting on the incarnation of the Word in space and time. Theologians use it as a quarry for abstract ideas about Christ and reality without reading the text as a whole and in its context.

- *canonical:* These dangers can be avoided by reading John's Gospel as part of the church's canon (authoritative collection) of Scripture. John is not the only Gospel or the only New Testament approach to Jesus. It must be placed alongside the other books of the Bible. The present text, whole and entire, is the canonical version of John's Gospel. One cannot pick and choose among its sayings to bolster peculiar positions in theology and practice.

- *spiritual:* Since the late second century, John has been known as the "spiritual" Gospel. That word carries a variety of nuances. John's Gospel challenges its readers to be on the side of the "spirit" as opposed to that of the "flesh." It speaks to a community of believers animated and guided by the Spirit-Paraclete. It presents the challenges of Jesus' person and teaching, which must always be the foundation of every sound Christian spirituality.

Outline of Contents

I. Introduction (1:1-51)

Prologue (1:1-18)
John the Baptist's Witness About Himself (1:19-28)
John the Baptist's Witness About Jesus (1:29-34)
The First Disciples (1:35-42)
The Calls of Philip and Nathanael (1:43-51)

II. Jesus' Public Signs and Speeches (2:1—12:50)

The Wedding at Cana (2:1-12)
Cleansing of the Temple (2:13-25)
Jesus and Nicodemus (3:1-21)
The Final Witness of John the Baptist (3:22-30)
The One from Above (3:31-36)
Jesus and the Samaritan Woman (4:1-42)
Jesus Heals the Official's Son (4:43-54)
Jesus and the Sabbath (5:1-47)
Feeding of the Five Thousand (6:1-15)
The Walking on Water (6:16-25)
Bread of Life Discourse (6:26-71)
Jesus at Tabernacles (7:1-52)
The Woman Taken in Adultery (7:53-8:11)
Light of the World (8:12-20)
Statements, Misunderstandings, Corrections (8:21-59)
The Man Born Blind (9:1-41)
The Good Shepherd (10:1-21)
Jesus at Hanukkah (10:22-42)
The Raising of Lazarus (11:1-44)
The Plot Against Jesus (11:45-57)
Anointing at Bethany and Entry into Jerusalem (12:1-19)
The End of Jesus' Public Ministry (12:20-50)

III. Jesus' Farewells to His Disciples (13:1-17:27)

The Footwashing (13:1-20)
Prophecies of Betrayal and the
  New Commandment (13:21-38)
Assurances and Promises (14:1-31)
Love and Hate (15:1-16:4)
Jesus' Departure and Return (16:5-33)
The Prayer of God's Son (17:1-26)

IV. The "Hour" of Jesus (18:1-21:25)

The Arrest of Jesus (18:1-27)
The Trial before Pilate (18:28-19:16)
The Death of Jesus (19:17-42)
Easter Faith (20:1-31)
Appendix: Peter and the Beloved Disciple (21:1-25)

I

Introduction (1:1-51)

Prologue (1:1-18)

In drama a "prologue" is an introductory speech, often in verse, that calls attention to the major themes of a play. John 1:1-18 fits this definition of a prologue. Much of the text follows the standards of biblical poetry: short units in parallel lines, and movement by association of words ("staircase parallelism"). It introduces the major ideas developed in the body of the Gospel: Jesus has cosmic significance; as a historical figure he was rejected by some and accepted by some; his task was to reveal his heavenly Father; he was able to make people the children of God and thus share his special relationship with the Father; his presence among us was the manifestation of God's glory.

The prologue probably incorporates parts of an early Christian hymn (1:1-5, 10-14, 16), though there is no unanimity about the precise extent of that hymn. Some of the terms that are prominent in the fragments of the hymn (Jesus as the "Word," the "tabernacling" of the Word in 1:14, "fullness" and "grace" in 1:16) are not developed as the Gospel proceeds. But most of the hymn and what has been added to fill it out are very appropriate as an introduction to John's story of Jesus. The prologue orients us to grasp who Jesus is and why he is important.

Two parts of the prologue (1:6-8; 1:15) concern John the Baptist. They are written in prose rather than poetry. Using these two pieces of prose as an entry, one can discern the following structure in the present text of John 1:1-18: A—the Word's place (1:1-5); B—John's witness (1:6-8); C—the Light's journey (1:9-11); D—empowerment by the Word (1:12-13); C1—the Word's journey (1:14); B1—John's witness (1:15); A1—the Word's place (1:16-18). This parallel structure that highlights the ideas in the center (chiasmus) is common in John's Gospel, as the exposition below will show. Its appearance in the prologue prepares for its many uses elsewhere.

Behind the identification of Jesus as the Word of God is the biblical portrayal of Wisdom as a personal figure. According to Proverbs 8:22-26 Wisdom existed before the world was created:

> The Lord begot me, the firstborn of
>   his ways.
>   the forerunner of his prodigies of
>   long ago;
> From of old I was poured forth,
>   at the first, before the earth.
> When there were no depths I was
>   brought forth,
>   when there were no fountains or
>   springs of water;
> Before the mountains were settled
>   into place,
>   before the hills, I was brought
>   forth;
> While as yet the earth and the fields
>   were not made,
>   nor the first clods of the world.

Sirach 24:8-12 describes Wisdom's dwelling in Israel, with God's people:

> Then the Creator of all gave me his
>   command,
>   and he who formed me chose the
>   spot for my tent,

Saying, 'In Jacob make your dwelling,
 in Israel your inheritance.'
Before all ages, in the beginning, he
 created me,
  and through all ages I shall not
  cease to be.
In the holy tent I ministered before
 him,
  and in Zion I fixed my abode.
Thus in the chosen city he has given
 me rest,
  in Jerusalem is my domain.
I have struck root among the glorious
 people,
  in the portion of the Lord, his
  heritage.

Wisdom 7:25-26 characterizes Wisdom as the one who reveals God:

For she is an aura of the might of
 God
  and a pure effusion of the glory of
  the Almighty;
  therefore nought that is sullied
  enters into her.
For she is the refulgence of eternal
 light,
  the spotless mirror of the power of
  God,
  the image of his goodness.

The first part of the prologue (1:1-5) describes the Word of God before creation (1:1-2) and in creation (1:3-5). The phrase "in the beginning" deliberately recalls the opening words of the book of Genesis. The application of "Word" to Jesus recalls the creative power of God's word according to Genesis 1. There may also be some connection to the idea of the Word (Logos) of God as a mediator between God and creation that was developed especially by Philo of Alexandria, a first-century Jewish writer who tried to join the Old Testament and Greek philosophy. But the most important piece of background is the Jewish portrayal of Wisdom as a personal figure who assisted God at the creation (see Proverbs 8; Wisdom 7; Sirach 24). As the Wisdom of God, Jesus was in the beginning with God. But the prologue to John's Gospel goes beyond its Old Testament models first by calling Jesus the "Word" and then by affirming his divinity ("and the Word was God"). Throughout the Gospel, Jesus, by word and action, reveals his heavenly Father. As God's Word, he communicates what was on God's mind to reveal. The Gospel reaches its climax when Thomas correctly identifies the risen Jesus as "my Lord and my God" (20:28). As God's agent in creation (1:3), the Word was responsible for "life" and "light"—fitting terms for the one who is the life (11:25) and the light (8:12) in his public ministry. The contrast between light and darkness (1:5) not only recalls the creation story (Gen 1:3-5), but also sets the stage for Jesus' struggle on behalf of the children of light against the powers of darkness. From the opening of the prologue, we learn about the identity of Jesus, his cosmic significance, and the conflict that will shape his life on earth.

The first prose piece (1:6-8) puts John the Baptist in his place as a witness to Jesus. Although John, like Jesus (4:34), was sent by God, he came to bear witness to Jesus the light. This definition of John's role as a witness to Jesus prepares for the more extensive developments of the theme in 1:19-42 and 3:22-30. In the background may be claims about John the Baptist put forward by those who kept alive John's movement and viewed Jesus as a rival.

The description of the coming of the Light into the world (1:9-11) gives particular attention to the negative reception that Jesus received from the world and his own people. Sent by God to reveal God, Jesus is the "man from heaven." But neither the "world" nor "his own people" accept him (1:11). Of course, the earliest followers of Jesus were Jews, and so "his own people" means "most" or "many" of his own people, not all without exception. Throughout the Gospel, the chief Jewish opponents of Jesus are called the "Jews." The idea of opposition to Jesus from his own people is expressed already in the prologue.

The coming of God's Son into the world made it possible for others to become children of God (1:12-13) through faith. This new status must be viewed as God's gift rather than a right or an acquisition. Some ancient manuscripts read the verb in 1:13 as a singular ("who was born") and make the sentence into a reference to Jesus' virginal conception ("who was born not by natural generation . . . but of God").

The second description of the Word's coming into the world (1:14) uses two powerful images: incarnation ("became flesh") and "tabernacling" ("made his dwelling"). Without ceasing to be or being any less, the Word became also "flesh" (see 1 John 4:2; 2 John 7). The tabernacle or tent of meeting in Exod 25:8-9 was the place of God's presence among the people of Israel. Whereas the first description of the Word's coming stressed the negative reception from the world and from the "Jews," the second description focuses on the positive reception ("we saw his glory"). The terms "grace and truth" describe the covenant relationship between God and his people (Exod 34:6). As God's only Son, Jesus is the full manifestation of God's glory that had only been glimpsed previously in Israel's history.

The second prose passage about John the Baptist (1:15) is a preview of what John says in 1:30: Even though Jesus came after John in time, he outranks John because, as the Word of God, he existed before John. Thus the superiority of Jesus is traced backward to the pre-existence of the Word.

The place of the Word in the history of salvation is taken up again in 1:16-18. The covenant with Moses was a "grace," and the Law through Moses to Israel was a gift. Without rejecting those gifts, the prologue insists that Jesus Christ was a "grace on top of grace" (1:16) and that he brought about the "grace and truth" between God and his people that was the goal of the covenant. In the body of the Gospel, Jesus neither annuls nor replaces the Scriptures. Rather, they reach their fullness in him (see 5:39). The chief function of the Word is to reveal God (1:18): "The only Son, God, who is at the Father's side, has revealed him." While John perceived the Father and the Son as distinct, he ascribed deity to both (see 1:1; 20:28). The Son is now back with ("in the bosom of") the Father. The task of the Son on earth was to reveal God to human beings and so to open up the way toward the Father. How he fulfilled that task is the topic of the body of John's Gospel.

The prologue has told us who Jesus is and why he is important. As one reads John's Gospel, it is helpful to keep going back to the themes and images of John 1:1-18 to put what is happening in its proper perspective. That is the prologue's function.

John the Baptist's Witness About Himself (1:19-28)

The prologue at two points emphasizes the role of John the Baptist as a witness to Jesus (1:6-8, 15). In the first two episodes of the Gospel narrative, John expresses agreement with the subordinate place given to him there ("He was not the light, but came to testify to the light," 1:8). He first explains that he was not the light by bearing witness about himself (1:19-28). Then he testifies to the light by giving testimony about Jesus (1:29-34).

John's witness about himself consists of two scenes (1:19-23, 24-28) in which a question is put to John (1:19, 22; 1:24-25) and John responds to it (1:20-21, 23; 1:26-27). The final verse locates the conversations in Bethany (Bethabara in some manuscripts), on the east side of the Jordan River.

The first set of questioners are experts in rituals—priests and Levites sent to John by the "Jews" (or Judeans) from Jerusalem. Throughout the Gospel, the "Jews" appear as the chief opponents of Jesus. Rather than representing the entire Jewish people, the "Jews" appear as the leadership based in Jerusalem that is hostile to Jesus. The question put to John by the emissaries of the Jews is, "Who are you?" (1:19). John first denies that he is one of the great figures expected by Israel in the future: the Messiah (2 Samuel 7), Elijah (Mal 3:23), or the Prophet like Moses (Deut 18:15). The readers of the Gospel believe that Jesus has filled these three roles. When pressed to define his own role, John appeals to Isaiah 40:3: He is "the voice of one crying in the desert, 'Make straight the way of the Lord'" (1:23).

The second set of questioners (1:24) are Pharisees, the Jewish religious sect that, in John's Gospel, is related to or even synonymous with the "Jews." They want to know why John baptizes at all (1:25). John's answer is based on a saying found in the other Gospels (Mark 1:7; Matt 3:11; Luke 3:16), in which John points toward the superiority of "the one who is coming after me" (1:27). That one is so superior that John is not worthy to do for him what a slave would do for his master—to loosen his sandal strap.

The first episode in the Gospel subordinates John to Jesus: Jesus is the one to come, and John is merely his witness. It also introduces the chief opponents of Jesus: the "Jews" and/or the Pharisees. Right from the start, they do not understand the real identity of Jesus: "There is one among you whom you do not recognize" (1:26). It prepares for John's testimony about Jesus in the next episode.

John the Baptist's Witness About Jesus (1:29-34)

John's testimony about Jesus takes place "on the next day" (see 1:35, 43). His audience is not specified. It could be the opponents from the preceding episode, or his disciples from the following episode, or some other group. John the Baptist recounts the events surrounding the baptism of Jesus. Whereas the other Evangelists narrate this event directly (Mark 1:9-11; Matt 3:13-17; Luke 3:21-22), John has John the Baptist look back on a past event and draw out the significance of that event.

Because John's story of Jesus' baptism is so similar to what appears in the other Gospels, the reader may miss the distinctive approach taken in the Fourth Gospel. John's witness to Jesus occurs in two segments: Jesus is the Lamb of God and the pre-existent one (1:29-31), and the Spirit-bearer and the Son of God (1:32-34).

Jesus is the Lamb of God (1:29)—a title that surely evoked the image of the Passover Lamb (Exodus 12) that was sacrificed in the Jerusalem temple on the afternoon before the start of the Passover festival. The sacrifice of the Passover Lamb coincided with Jesus' death on Good Friday according to John's chronology (see John 18:28; 19:31, 42). The emphasis on the expiatory character of the Lamb's activity ("who takes away the sin of the world") connects Jesus with the Suffering Servant of Isaiah 53. The real reason for Jesus' superiority over John the Baptist is expressed with reference to Jesus' pre-existence ("who ranks ahead of me because he existed before me," 1:30), which was already made clear in the prologue (1:1-3, 15). Even the rationale for John's baptism is related to Jesus; it was to make Jesus manifest to Israel (1:31).

In the second segment (1:32-34), John the Baptist tells about the baptism of Jesus. He makes no connection with the forgiveness of sins and repentance (Mark 1:4), and shows no embarrassment about baptizing Jesus (see Matt 3:14-15). The reason is that the whole purpose of John's baptism is to manifest Jesus to Israel (1:31). Jesus is the bearer of the Holy Spirit. Not only does the Spirit descend upon Jesus, but also the Spirit "abides" or "remains" upon him (1:32, 33)—a key word in the Johannine vocabulary. The reference to Jesus as baptizing in the Holy Spirit looks forward not so much to his own baptizing activity (3:22; 4:1-2) as to his death and resurrection (7:39; 19:30; 20:22).

John the Baptist's testimony to Jesus concludes with the title "Son of God"—the most important way of referring to Jesus in this Gospel. Whereas in the other Gospels, the title is supplied by the voice from heaven ("you are/this is my Son"), here John the Baptist presents it as his own opinion, too ("I have seen and testified").

John's testimony about himself defined and limited his role as subordinate to Jesus. His testimony about Jesus shows why that subordination was necessary. Modern scholars sometimes detect behind these texts tension between followers of John the Baptist and Jesus' disciples, and maintain that the goal of John 1:19-34 is to put John in his proper place. Whatever polemical elements may be behind these texts, their present thrust is to identify Jesus as Lamb of God, Suffering Servant, the preexistent one, the Spirit-bearer, and the Son of God.

The First Disciples (1:35-42)

On the next day (see 1:29), John the Baptist identifies Jesus as the Lamb of God (1:36) to two of his disciples, one of whom is later named as Andrew (1:40). Thus the first disciples of Jesus come from the circle of John the Baptist and on the strength of John's own recommendation. Jesus' first words to these would-be followers ("What are you looking for?", 1:38) form an appropriate prelude not only for the disciple-stories in chapter one, but also for the entire Gospel. The first disciples address Jesus as "Rabbi" (teacher), thus supplying still another title. The text introduces Jesus and the first disciples and so moves the story of Jesus on stage. Up to this point, the narrator and John the Baptist had been speaking about Jesus. It also provides the vocabulary of discipleship: follow (1:37, 38), look for or seek (1:38), stay or abide (1:38, 39), and see (1:39).

In Mark 1:16-18, Andrew and Simon follow Jesus spontaneously in response to his summons by the Sea of Galilee. In this Gospel, the call of the first two disciples apparently occurs in Bethany (1:28, 43). They act first on John's recommendation and seek Jesus out. The first step in their discipleship is "abiding" (1:38, 39) with Jesus. The concluding note that all this took place about the tenth hour (4:00 P.M.) has no obvious symbolic value. Some interpreters place the incident late Friday afternoon and assume that Andrew and his companion spent the entire Sabbath "abiding" with Jesus.

Just as John's witness brought Andrew to Jesus (1:35-39), so Andrew brings Simon Peter to Jesus (1:40-42). After announcing that Jesus is the Messiah (1:41; see 1:20, 25), Andrew introduces him to Jesus, who promptly gives Simon son of John the nickname "Peter" ("Rocky"), presumably because of some personal characteristic (see Matt 16:18 for a different reason). Jesus knows his disciples from the start.

In the course of the text, three Hebrew (or Aramaic) words are given translations: Rabbi (teacher), Messiah (anointed), and Kephas (Peter=Rocky). All these prove is that the Evangelist was writing in Greek for readers who understood Greek. To argue that he used a Semitic source or that he wrote for non-Jews goes beyond the evidence.

The story of the first disciples adds to the picture of Jesus: He is Rabbi and Messiah as well as Lamb of God. It indicates that even the first followers came to Jesus in response to the witness of others. It provides the vocabulary of discipleship (seeking, following, seeing) and defines discipleship as "abiding" (staying) with Jesus.

The Calls of Philip and Nathanael (1:43-51)

The next disciple to be called (1:43-44) is Philip from Bethsaida, a small fishing village on the northeast corner of the Sea of Galilee (see 12:21) that had been raised to the dignity of a city before 2 B.C. It is said to have been the town of Andrew and Peter. The story of Philip's call is simple, like those in Mark 1:16-20 and 2:14: "And Jesus said to him, 'Follow me.'"

Philip in turn recruits Nathanael (1:45-51). In his conversation with Nathanael (1:45-46), Philip adds to the portrait of Jesus as the one who fulfills the Scriptures and identifies Jesus (from only an earthly perspective) as Joseph's son and as from Nazareth in Galilee. In response to Nathanael's cynical dismissal of Nazareth, Philip extends the invitation of Jesus to Andrew and the other disciple: "Come and see" (1:46; see 1:39). Nathanael is not mentioned in the lists of Jesus' twelve disciples, though he is sometimes identified as Bartholomew. Situated on a main road and said to have had a population of 2,000 persons in Jesus' time, Nazareth was not especially obscure. And so the grounds for its dismissal here are not obvious.

From his personal experience of Jesus (1:47-51), Nathanael learns that Jesus' earthly origins do not explain him entirely. As was the case with Peter (1:42), Jesus shows that he knew all about Nathanael before he ever met him. As a true Israelite without duplicity (1:47), Nathanael stands in contrast to Jacob, the first to be called "Israel" (Gen 32:29) and well known for his duplicity (Gen 27:35) with Isaac and Esau. For the fig tree as a symbol of peaceful existence, see Mic 4:4; Zech 3:10. Jesus' remarkable foreknowledge of Nathanael leads him to add two more titles: Son of God (the central title in the Gospel that stresses Jesus' unique relationship to the Father), and King of Israel (which prepares for the passion narrative in which Jesus is condemned as King of the Jews).

For the final title ("Son of Man") in 1:51, Jesus shifts to the plural ("you will see"). There is an allusion to Jacob's dream in Gen 28:12: "A stairway (or ladder) rested on the ground, with its top reaching to the heavens; and God's messengers were going up and down on it." Here Jesus the Son of Man is a glorious figure, the locus of divine glory and the point of contact between heaven and earth.

With all the titles in chapter one, we get a clear idea of who Jesus is. The traditional titles applied to Jesus have been introduced. We also learn about following Jesus—its dynamics, vocabulary, and essence.

II

Jesus' Public Signs and Speeches (2:1-12:50)

The Wedding at Cana (2:1-12)

Jesus' changing water into wine at the wedding in Cana is called the "beginning of his signs" (2:11). As such, it is the first in the series of seven signs (see 4:46-54; 5:1-9; 6:1-15, 16-21; 9:1-12; 11:1-44), miraculous actions that manifest the glory of Jesus during his earthly ministry. The key to the Cana episode and to all the signs appears in Jesus' statement to his mother: "My hour has not yet come" (2:4). In John's Gospel, the "hour" of Jesus includes his passion, death, resurrection, and ascension (see 13:1). Only in these events, which are understood as the exaltation of Jesus, is the glory of Jesus really shown forth. Thus the miracles or "signs" done during Jesus' earthly ministry must be taken as anticipations or previews of the fullness of his glory. On the other hand, the signs point forward to the "hour" of Jesus' passion, death, resurrection, and exaltation.

The wedding takes place in Cana of Galilee (2:1), usually identified by scholars as Khirbet Qanah, a deserted site about 5½ miles northwest of Kefar Kenna. The reference to the "third day," which does not fit the sequence developed in chapter one, has been interpreted in various ways (Tuesday as the Jewish marriage day, a symbol of Jesus' resurrection, etc.) without any certainty having been reached. The guests include not only Jesus and his disciples (2:2), but also the "mother of

Jesus" (her usual title in John's Gospel where she is never called Mary). A crisis emerges when there is no wine (2:3). Such a happening would bring shame upon the hosts in a culture in which honor and reputation were valued highly.

When the mother of Jesus brings the lack of wine to Jesus' attention (2:3), Jesus' initial response (2:4) seems cold and even insulting: "Woman, how does your concern affect me?" The address "woman" is polite (see 20:15) but unusual in speaking to one's mother (see 19:26-27). The question is a biblical idiom (see Judg 11:12; 2 Sam 19:23; 1 Kgs 17:18; 2 Kgs 3:13; etc.) that suggests some distance between people ("That's not my problem"). The reason for Jesus' hesitation is explained by his statement: "My hour has not yet come."

Yet the mother of Jesus has faith that her son will do whatever is needed to save the day. So she tells the servants: "Do whatever he tells you" (2:5). Jesus acts in response to Mary's faith in his power, not because of the embarrassment of the hosts or even Mary's physical relationship to him.

The miracle is told indirectly (2:6-10). The six stone (see Lev 11:29-38) jars, each holding "two or three measures" (twenty to thirty gallons), are filled with water on Jesus' command to the servants. When the official managing the banquet draws from the jars, he finds excellent wine rather than water and wonders where it came from (2:9), thus providing an example of ignorance about Jesus and his origins. The custom of serving good wine first (2:10) is otherwise unknown.

The biblical background of Jesus' changing water into wine is best sought in texts about Wisdom's banquet in Prov 9:2, 5: "She (=Wisdom) mixed her wine...'Come, eat of my food, and drink of the wine I have mixed!'" The episode also recalls the image of abundant wine in the last days (Isa 25:6; Jer 31:12; Amos 9:13-14; Hos 14:8; etc.). Some scholars suggest an association with the cult of the Greek god, Dionysus, whose festivals featured the consumption of wine.

In 1:50 Jesus promised Nathanael: "You will see greater things than this." The "greater things" include the signs done by Jesus in which his glory is revealed and in response to which his disciples believe in him (2:11). Some find additional symbolic messages in this first sign. One line of interpretation sees the good wine supplied by Jesus as replacing the Jewish waters of purification (see 2:6). Another approach identifies Jesus as the new wine embodied in the eucharistic celebrations of the church. Still another tradition of interpretation finds in Jesus' presence at Cana his blessing upon the institution of marriage.

In the other Gospels, the center of Jesus' ministry is Capernaum, on the Sea of Galilee. In John Jesus, his family, and his disciples stay there only a few days (2:12). This is the first mention of Jesus' "brothers" (see 7:3). In Hebrew, the term "brother" can refer to various male relatives (blood brother, half-brother, cousin, brother-in-law, etc.).

The sign at Cana points forward to Jesus' "hour" on the cross (19:25-37) and to the banquet in God's kingdom. The mother of Jesus shows perfect faith in Jesus from the start and thus deserves to be seen as the mother of all believers (19:26-27).

Cleansing of the Temple (2:13-25)

John places Jesus' cleansing of the temple on the first of three Passovers (2:13; 6:4; 13:1) that give structure to Jesus' public ministry. Passover commemorated Israel's escape from slavery in Egypt (see Exodus 11-15). Connected with the old agricultural celebration of Unleavened Bread, Passover was, in Jesus' time, a pilgrimage festival that attracted large crowds to the Jerusalem temple. It took place in the spring, in March or April. Thus Jesus goes up as one of many pilgrims to celebrate the liberation of his people in Jerusalem.

The cleansing of the temple (2:14-17) occurs in the area around the place of sacrifice and the Holy of Holies. This large courtyard featured places where pilgrims could buy animals for sacrifice and change money into the proper currency. At best, the merchants were providing services that were necessary for the smooth running of the temple. By accusing them of making the temple into a marketplace (2:16; see Zech 14:21), Jesus justifies his action in driving them out. The incident is also presented as the fulfillment of Ps 69:9 ("Zeal for your house will consume me"), which not only gives a basis for

Jesus' activity but also suggests a connection with Jesus' death.

John's account of the cleansing of the temple differs in many respects from those in the other Gospels (Mark 11:15-17; Matt 21:1-13; Luke 19:45-46). The most obvious difference is the time. In John it occurs early in Jesus' public ministry, whereas in the other Gospels, it takes place shortly before Jesus' death. Only in John does Jesus use a whip (2:15) and address the dovesellers directly (2:16). Whereas in the other Gospels, the biblical text is a combination of Isa 56:7 and Jer 7:11, here it is Ps 69:9.

But the most important difference comes in the interpretation given to Jesus' action (2:18-22): the dismantling of the temple system is a sign of Jesus' death and resurrection. The interpretation appears in a conversation between the "Jews" and Jesus. To their demand for a sign (2:18), Jesus answers with a saying that appears elsewhere in the New Testament (Matt 26:61; Mark 14:58; Acts 6:14): "Destroy this temple and in three days I will raise it up." Only in John is the saying directly connected with Jesus' death and resurrection ("he was speaking about the temple of his body," 2:21).

The dynamic of John 2:18-22 is typical of many dialogues in the Fourth Gospel. The questioners are the "Jews"—a group hostile to Jesus. Despite having just been given a sign in the form of Jesus cleansing the temple, they demand another "sign" that would justify Jesus' action (2:18). When Jesus talks about the sign of the temple (2:19), they misunderstand and imagine that he is talking about the massive remodeling of the Jerusalem temple begun by Herod the Great. The presence of the "Jews" as hostile questioners and their failure to understand Jesus are typical of the dialogues in the Fourth Gospel.

The misunderstanding on the part of the questioners leads the reader to greater clarity. Thus in the light of Jesus' death and resurrection, the disciples came to interpret Jesus' temple-saying as a prophecy of his resurrection (2:21-22). They also came to accept the Scriptures as a witness to Jesus and Jesus' own words.

By placing the cleansing of the temple at the beginning of Jesus' public activity in Jerusalem, John lodges a protest against the commercialization of the temple area and thus criticizes the temple system. He also foreshadows Jesus' death by quoting Ps 69:9: Zeal for God's temple will eventually destroy Jesus. Finally, he identifies the resurrected Jesus as the renewed and restored temple, thus suggesting that after the destruction of the Jerusalem temple in A.D. 70, the worship of the God of Israel is best carried on with reference to Jesus.

The summary about Jesus' ministry (2:23-25) in Jerusalem during the eight days of the Passover feast takes up the "Jews'" search for a sign and suggests the faith produced by Jesus' signs (2:23) was not adequate or appropriate. Thus we are prepared for the description of Nicodemus' approach to Jesus (3:2) and for Jesus' cool reception of him. The passage also carries on the theme of Jesus' extraordinary knowledge (see 1:48).

Jesus and Nicodemus (3:1-21)

The Nicodemus story in John 3:1-21 consists of a narrative (3:1-2a), a dialogue (3:2b-10), and a discourse (3:11-21). Whereas in the first part (3:1-10) Jesus confronts Nicodemus directly, in the second part (3:11-21) the discourse moves into the plural "you" and talks about Jesus in the third person.

The introductory narrative (3:1-2a) identifies Nicodemus as a Pharisee and "a ruler of the Jews." The basis for his interest in Jesus is the "signs" that he had done (3:2b). Thus Nicodemus is linked to Jesus' opponents (2:18) and to those whose belief Jesus did not fully approve (2:23). Nevertheless, subsequent mentions of Nicodemus in 7:50 and 19:39 indicate that Jesus' instruction had a positive effect in moving him from darkness ("he came to Jesus at night," 3:2) to the light.

The dialogue features quick exchanges between Jesus (3:3, 5-8, 10) and Nicodemus (3:4, 9). Jesus begins by declaring: "No one can see the kingdom of God without being born from above" (3:3). There may be some connection with Jesus' sayings found in Matt 18:3; Mark 10:15; Luke 18:17: "Unless one becomes like a child again, he cannot enter the kingdom of God." The mention of the "kingdom of God" appears only here and in 3:5 in John's Gospel. The key word, however, is the adverb translated "from above." The Greek word, *anōthen*, can mean both "from above" and "again." Nicodemus in 3:4 misunderstands it to mean "again" and objects that no one can be born again. His misunderstanding gives Jesus the opportunity to explain what being born "from above" means (3:5-8).

Being born "from above" makes living in the spirit possible. The fundamental opposition is between flesh (the realm of weakness and mortality) and spirit (the realm of divine power and life). One who has been born "from above" (from God) lives in the realm of the spirit under the guidance of the Holy Spirit. The word for "spirit/Spirit" in Greek and Hebrew is the same as that for "wind." The analogy in 3:8 about the mysterious activity of the wind ("the wind blows where it will") highlights the mysterious activity of God's grace.

In 3:5 Jesus talks about being born of "water and Spirit." In light of the basic oppositions in 3:5-8 (flesh-spirit, below-above), the meaning of "spirit/Spirit" is clear. But what does "water" mean? It is usually taken as a reference to baptism involving water and the gift of the Holy Spirit. Some scholars attribute the word "water" to a later editor who sought to bring the text in line with church theology and practice. Others take it as a reference to the natural process of birth, either to seminal fluid or to the waters of the womb. Still others take it as another image for "from above" (the rain) or for cleansing (as in Ezek 36:25).

The conversation trails away in 3:9-10 when Nicodemus expresses amazement ("How can this happen?"), and Jesus wonders how a teacher (see 3:2) in Israel could misunderstand him. The thrust of the conversation so far is the need to live "from above," which is in the spirit/Spirit. To interpret it as meaning "born again" is to repeat Nicodemus' misunderstanding.

The conversation turns into a discourse in 3:11-21. It is not always clear who is speaking and who is addressed. At a few points, Jesus ("I" in 3:11-12) speaks. But more often he is spoken about, and sometimes the speaker is "we." Nicodemus has dropped from sight, and most of the "you" language is plural. Now we seem to have a conversation between the Johannine community ("we speak of what we know and we testify to what we have seen") and their Jewish opponents ("but you people do not accept our testimony," 3:11).

The opponents do not yet understand "heavenly things" because they do not accept the "man from heaven"—Jesus the Son of Man (3:13-15) and Son of God (3:16). As in 1:51, the Son of Man is a glorious figure who mediates between heaven and earth. The description in 3:13 ("No one else has gone up to heaven") seems to assume that the resurrection has already occurred. Whereas ascents to heaven were claimed for other figures (Enoch, Moses, Elijah), this text limits the heavenly ascent to the one who first came down from heaven. Just as Moses saved the people from death by lifting up the bronze serpent (Num 21:8-9), so the lifting up of the Son of Man first on the cross and then in the resurrection/ascension has made eternal life possible for those who believe in him (3:14-15).

John 3:16 ("God so loved the world...") is a good summary of the entire Gospel. It identifies Jesus as the Son of God whose death was the high point of his mission from the Father and a sign of God's love for the world. Those who believe in him may have eternal life (which has already begun). Many Jews and early Christians believed that judgment and eternal life belonged to the end of human history. For John, these end-time events had been anticipated through Jesus' death and resurrection. The criterion for judgment is belief (or unbelief) in God's Son Jesus (3:18), and for believers the end-time reward of eternal life has already begun.

In the prologue (1:5, 9), Jesus was described as the light shining in the darkness and coming into the world. The idea of faith in Jesus as the criterion for judgment is developed in 3:19-21. There are two kinds of people: The children of darkness do evil deeds, while the children of light "do the truth." Here a Jewish pattern found in some Dead Sea scrolls (see *Manual of Discipline* 3-4) is adapted to fit the Christian conviction that, with the coming of the Light (Jesus) into the world, the final judgment had already taken place. The text also describes those who believe in Jesus as "doing the truth" (3:21). Truth is a dynamic reality, something that remains to be done. It is not simply something to be thought about or admired.

Dualistic thinking divides people and all reality into two camps: good and evil, light and darkness, etc. The Qumran *Manual of Discipline,* cols. 3—4, provides a good example of Jewish dualistic thinking. Acknowledging the ultimate sovereignty of God, it proceeds to divide all creation in two:

> He has created man to govern the world, and has appointed for him two spirits in which to walk until the time of His visitation: the spirits of truth and falsehood. Those born of truth spring from a fountain of light, but those born of falsehood spring from a source of darkness. All the children of righteousness are ruled by the Prince of Light and walk in the ways of light, but all the children of falsehood are ruled by the Angel of Darkness and walk in the ways of darkness.

Many familiar oppositions emerge in John 3:1-21: from above-from below, spirit-flesh, heavenly-earthly, and light-darkness. The promise of final judgment and hope for eternal life were part of (some) Jewish theology in the first century. The major innovation in John is the insistence on the centrality of Jesus and the claim that, through him, the judgment and the reward have already taken place.

The Final Witness of John the Baptist (3:22-30)

The story of Jesus' public ministry began with the witness of John the Baptist (1:19-36). Now it returns for a final testimony from John. After describing the baptisms being administered by Jesus and John (3:22-24), the text sets the stage (3:25-26) for one last effort at clarifying the relationship between the two figures (3:27-30).

Only the Fourth Gospel states that Jesus baptized (3:22; compare 4:1-2); there are good reasons to assume that he was perceived as the disciple and extension of John the Baptist. In fact, the thrust of both 1:19-36 and 3:22-30 is to affirm the ultimate superiority of Jesus. Since Jesus was already in Jerusalem, the point of 3:22 ("went into the region of Judea") is that he traveled elsewhere in Judean territory. The precise location of Aenon near Salim (3:23) is unknown; it is usually placed near Beth-shean or Shechem, and by the Jordan River. It is presented as the center of John's ministry before his arrest. The apparent competition between Jesus and John is the occasion for the final witness of John.

The proximate occasion is a dispute between John's disciples and "a Jew about ceremonial washings" (3:25). Nothing is ever made out of the ceremonial washings as the story proceeds. And one would expect the other partner in debate to have been Jesus or his disciples. The complaint of John's disciples is that Jesus is becoming too popular: "here he is baptizing, and everyone is coming to him" (3:26).

Jesus' growing popularity does not disturb John because all is in God's hands (3:27b). He recalls his previous testimony that he was not the Messiah (1:20) but rather was sent beforehand (1:23). Then he compares himself to the "best man" at a wedding, the one who took care of arranging the wedding ceremonies and celebrations (3:29). The "best man" does not compete with the groom; his task is to make things run smoothly and well. The image not only assigns a subordinate role to John, but it also identifies Jesus as the messianic bridegroom (see Mark 2:19; Matt 9:15; Luke 5:35). John sees Jesus' career on the rise and his own on the wane (3:30).

Whereas the first witness of John to Jesus (1:19-36) served to introduce and identify Jesus, the final witness (3:22-30) prepares for John's own departure and emphasizes John's role as a subordinate (rather than a competitor) to Jesus.

The One from Above (3:31-36)

Who is speaking to whom? Though it is possible to take 3:31-36 as the continuation of John the Baptist's final witness, it is probably better to understand it as the comment of the Evangelist or of the Johannine community (which amounts to the same thing) as in 3:11-21. The paragraph summarizes the earlier parts of chapter three and provides the outline for the message of the entire Gospel.

Jesus comes "from above" or "from heaven" (3:31) and so is above all earthly things. His witness to heaven meets rejection (3:32; see 1:11) and some acceptance (3:33; see 1:12). His mission is to reveal God's words (3:34) and to pour out God's Spirit without measure. The text ends by asserting two favorite Johannine themes: the Father's love for the Son and his handing over all things to the Son, and belief in Jesus as the criterion of the (anticipated) last judgment.

This text provides a sketch of Johannine Christology: Jesus the Son of God the Father comes from and returns to the Father; the Father has sent the Son to reveal the Father; the Father loves the Son and has given all things over to him; and the Son has made the Father known (see Matt 11:27; Luke 10:22).

Jesus and the Samaritan Woman (4:1-42)

The first of several lengthy episodes in the Fourth Gospel features an encounter between Jesus and a woman from Samaria. Many outlines to illustrate the movement of the text have been proposed. Though differing in details, they usually place Jesus' statements about true worship (4:20-26) at the center and thus in the most prominent position.

After a narrative introduction (4:1-4), the episode of the Samaritan woman can be divided as follows: A—Jesus and the Samaritan woman (4:5-9); B—living water (4:10-15); C—Jesus' witness about the Samaritan woman (4:16-19); D—true worship (4:20-26); C1—the Samaritan woman's witness about Jesus (4:27-30); B1—true food (4:31-38); A1—Jesus and the Samaritans (4:39-42).

The narrative introduction (4:1-4) explains what Jesus was doing in Samaria. Jesus' growing success in making disciples and baptizing apparently aroused the hostility of the Pharisees in Judea. In order to return to Galilee (see 4:44) from Judea, Jesus had to pass through Samaria. In fact, many Jews took another route to avoid Samaritan territory. The note of necessity most likely alludes to the divine plan that Jesus the revealer of God should be active even in Samaria. The comment that

Jesus did not baptize (4:2; see 3:22) may have been designed to rebut the claim that Jesus was only a follower and imitator of John the Baptist.

The encounter between Jesus and the Samaritan woman (4:5-9) takes place at Sychar, a village in or near biblical Shechem, near the land that Jacob gave to Joseph (see Gen 33:18-19; 48:22; Josh 24:32). The description of the place as Jacob's well (4:6) prepares for the woman's question in 4:12: "Are you greater than our father Jacob?" The observation that Jesus was "tired from his journey" (4:6) is one of the few admissions of his human weakness in the Fourth Gospel. The encounter begins when Jesus asks the woman for a drink of water (4:7). Her surprise at his question (4:9) may reflect the general estrangement between Judeans (and Galileans) and Samaritans that passed through various phases from Solomon's time onward. Or it may refer more narrowly to the Jewish conviction that the vessels of the Samaritans were ritually impure. In either case, Jesus is clearly identified here as a Jew (*Ioudaios*), thus preparing for his own assertion that salvation is from the Jews (4:22).

The conversation about "living water" (4:10-15) employs the familiar Johannine device of misunderstanding. Jesus uses the symbol of living water to refer to the revelation of God that he gives to human beings. The Samaritan woman imagines that "living water" is the running (non-stagnant) water in the well. She wonders how Jesus can supply such water without his own bucket or ladle (4:11) and ironically asks if he is greater than Jacob (4:12). From the perspective of John and his community, Jesus is indeed greater than Jacob. Her misunderstanding leads Jesus in 4:13-14 to contrast the effects of drinking from Jacob's well (thirst again) and from his living water (eternal life). The woman shows her continued misunderstanding with her hope that she would not have to return to the well (4:15).

Next (4:16-19) Jesus gives witness about the Samaritan woman's scandalous marital status (five husbands in the past and now a lover). This remarkable display of knowledge (see 1:47-50; 2:23-25) leads her to acknowledge Jesus as a prophet, which may allude to the Taheb, the restorer-prophet like Moses (see Deut 18:15) expected to restore the fortunes of the Samaritans (see 4:25).

Jesus' statements on true worship (4:20-26) constitute the center of the text. A major feature in the split between Jews and Samaritans involved the proper place of worship. Whereas Jews (and Galileans) worshiped in Jerusalem at Mount Zion, Samaritans worshiped in Shechem at Mount Gerizim. Even when John Hyrcanus destroyed the sanctuary at Mount Gerizim in 128 B.C., the Samaritans continued to worship there.

In this dispute, Jesus sides with the Jews, since he himself is a Jew (4:9) and contends that salvation is from the Jews (4:22). Nevertheless, he envisions an "hour" when worship at both sanctuaries will be replaced by "worship in Spirit and truth" (4:24). The statement "the hour is coming, and is now here" (4:23) may imply that the time is future from the perspective of the earthly Jesus and present from the perspective of the Johannine community. When the woman talks about the coming Messiah, Jesus in 4:26 accepts this identification: "I am he, the one who is speaking with you."

For the Johannine Christians after A.D. 70, this central statement (4:20-26) gave expression to their claim to carry on the proper worship of God after the destruction of the Jerusalem temple. The hour is here for worship in Spirit and truth.

Now the Samaritan woman bears witness to Jesus (4:27-30). When the disciples come back on the scene (4:27), they are surprised that Jesus was talking to this woman but do not express their wonderment. The woman in turn serves as a kind of missionary by going to the city and bearing witness to Jesus because of his remarkable knowledge of her life and his possible identity as the Messiah (4:29). Her witness brings the townspeople to Jesus (4:30).

The conversation about the "true food" (4:31-38) also employs the device of misunderstanding. When Jesus announces that he has food (4:32), the disciples assume that he got food from some other source (4:33). Their misunderstanding gives Jesus the occasion to explain that his food is to do God's will and to finish his work (4:34).

Loosely connected with the talk about food are two popular sayings: "In four months the harvest will be here" (4:35); "One sows and another reaps" (4:37). The effect of the commentary on the first saying (4:35b-36) is to deny the long gap between planting and harvest: With Jesus' preaching, the seed quickly ripens into the harvest of eternal life. The commentary on the second saying (4:38) is more problematic: Who are the "others" who have done the work? There may be an allusion to the tradition contained in Acts 8:4-25 where Peter and John confirm Philip's preaching of the gospel.

The episode concludes when the Samaritans encounter Jesus (4:39). Having first accepted Jesus on the strength of the woman's testimony about his remarkable knowledge, their direct experience of "abiding" (4:40; see 1:38-39) with Jesus leads to a new level of faith that no longer needs another to witness about him. They proclaim him as "savior of the world"—a title used in reference to the Roman emperor and other benefactors of society. Whereas the woman wondered (skeptically) whether Jesus might be greater than Jacob, the townspeople confess him to be savior of the world.

At the heart of this episode is the affirmation about the Jewishness of Jesus (4:9) from whom salvation comes (4:22). Jesus stands as the first of those who worship God in Spirit and truth. His example serves as the model for Jewish Christians after the destruction of the Jerusalem temple in A.D. 70.

Jesus Heals the Official's Son (4:43-54)

Jesus' second "sign" involves the healing at a distance of an official's son. Like the first sign (2:1-12), it takes place in Cana of Galilee (4:46). After describing Jesus' arrival in Galilee (4:43-45), John recounts the healing in 4:46-54.

After spending two days with the Samaritans (4:40), Jesus returns to Galilee. John explains Jesus' movements on the grounds that "a prophet has no honor in his native place" (4:44). Whereas in the other Gospels the saying refers to Nazareth (see Mark 6:4; Matt 13:57; Luke 4:24), in John the "native place" of Jesus where he is rejected is Jerusalem in Judea. Thus Jesus comes to Galilee because he feels rejected in Judea (see 4:1-3). On the other hand, the Galileans accept Jesus on the strength of what he had done in Jerusalem.

The healing of the official's son (4:46-54) has obvious connections with the healings of the centurion's son in Matt 8:5-13 and the centurion's servant in Luke 7:1-10. But there is debate whether John knew those texts or had access to an independent tradition. The chief difference is that in John Jesus remains in Cana and the son is in Capernaum, while in the other Gospels everything seems to take place in Capernaum.

The "official" was in the employ of the "king"—either the Roman emperor or Herod Antipas. It is not clear whether he is a Jew or a Gentile (see Luke 7:9). What is at issue is the nature of his faith. Jesus apparently criticizes "signs" faith (4:48), which believes only as a result of and in response to miracles. By accepting Jesus' word ("You may go; your son will live," 4:50), the official shows a superior kind of faith. By his action, he manifests his confidence that Jesus could heal at a distance by word alone.

The boy's condition is described in terms of life and death. He is said to be near death (4:47, 49). Jesus announces that the son will live (4:50, 53), and the announcement that greets the official is "your son will live" (4:52). The healing is a sign of Jesus' power over death and his ability to give life—a preview of the raising of Lazarus from the dead, which is the final sign in Jesus' public ministry. There is some irony in the fact that, as a result of the healing, the man and his whole household came to believe (4:53; see 4:48).

Jesus and the Sabbath (5:1-47)

The third sign done by Jesus—the healing at the pool of Bethesda—is the occasion for a long episode that locates Jesus with reference to the Sabbath. The chapter narrates the healing and the controversy generated by it (5:1-16), provides a discourse on Jesus' authority (5:17-30), and points to several witnesses regarding Jesus (5:31-47).

The third sign occurs at a pilgrimage feast (perhaps Weeks/Pentecost). Only at end of the narrative (5:10) and as a kind of afterthought are we told that it occurred on the Sabbath. The healing takes place in Jerusalem, north of the temple area, by the city gate through which sheep for sacrifice were brought in. The pool with five porticoes was an established spa or healing place; its remains have been excavated, showing that in several cases John's Gospel contains reliable information about places in ancient Palestine. The man had waited thirty-eight years at the healing place (5:5). The idea of an angel coming down to stir the waters appears only in late manuscripts at 5:3-4 and probably developed out of the man's own explanation in 5:7.

In their encounter (5:6-9), Jesus takes the initiative. He knows all about the man (5:6; see 1:48; 4:17-18) and invites him to be healed. He ignores the man's explanation why he could not enter the pool (5:7) and gives him a command to take up his mat and walk (5:8). The command and the verbal similarities with Mark 2:1-12 (see Matt 9:1-8; Luke 5:17-26) make one suspect that he had been paralyzed, though this is not said explicitly.

According to Leviticus 23:3 the Sabbath was set aside by God for worship and rest:

> For six days work may be done; but the seventh day is the sabbath rest, a day for sacred assembly, on which you shall do no work. The sabbath shall belong to the Lord wherever you dwell.

Rest involves abstaining from work. Mishnah *Shabbat* 7:2 provides a list of works that were judged to break the Sabbath rest:

> The main classes of work are forty save one: sowing, ploughing, reaping, binding sheaves, threshing, winnowing, cleansing crops, grinding, sifting, kneading, baking, shearing wool, washing or beating or dyeing it, spinning, weaving, making two loops, weaving two threads, separating two threads, tying [a knot], loosening [a knot], sewing two

[handwritten note: ⌐shoe laces?]

stitches, tearing in order to sew two stitches, hunting a gazelle, slaughtering or flaying or salting it or curing its skin, scraping it or cutting it up, writing two letters, erasing in order to write two letters, building, pulling down, putting out a fire, lighting a fire, striking with a hammer and taking out aught from one domain into another. These are the main classes of work: forty save one.

The comment that the healing took place on the Sabbath (5:9b) brings about a three-sided controversy among the "Jews," the man, and Jesus (5:10-18). Jesus' command ("take up your mat and walk," 5:8, 11-12) led the man to carry something from one domain to another and so constituted work in violation of the Sabbath rest. The "Jews" so focus on the Sabbath violation that they give no attention to the fact of the man's healing. Their real aim is to pursue Jesus. Jesus' advice to the man ("do not sin anymore, so that nothing worse may happen to you," 5:14) need not imply a causal connection between his former illness and his moral activity—a connection explicitly denied in John 9:3 with regard to the man born blind. Nor is there any need to interpret his telling the "Jews" that Jesus healed him (5:15) as a sinful act of treachery. At any rate, the Jews' quarrel is with Jesus. It concerns his loose attitude toward work on the Sabbath (5:16)—his own in healing a non-life-threatening illness, and the paralytic's carrying his mat from place to place.

Jesus' basic response to his opponents provides the "text" for the rest of the chapter: "My Father is at work until now, so I am at work" (5:17). In defending his actions, Jesus takes for granted the Jewish belief that, on the Sabbath, God continues to preserve his creation and to carry on the work of redemption. Jesus' answer not only appeals to his special relationship to God as his Father, but also claims equality with God (5:18). The thrust of Jesus' discourse in 5:19-30 is to show that this special relationship and equality implies no rivalry or alienation with respect to the Father.

The other Gospels base Jesus' free attitude toward the Sabbath rest on his claim that "the Son of Man is lord of the Sabbath" (Mark 2:28; Matt 12:8; Luke 6:5). Though that statement seems to be in the background of John, it is never said explicitly. Nevertheless, it is possible to understand John 5 as a reflection on its theological implications: As lord of the Sabbath, Jesus can and must do what God does; therefore, it is appropriate to call him Son of God and equal to the Father (5:18). Ironically, the "Jews" are exactly correct.

Jesus' defense of his authority (5:19-30) begins with a parable or analogy: A son learns from watching what his father does (5:19). The defense proper (5:20-29) is arranged chiastically (as in 4:4-42): A—Jesus applies the parable to his Father-Son relationship to God, and promises even "greater works" than healing a paralytic on the Sabbath (5:20); B—Jesus claims that the Father has given over to him as Son what is allowed for God to do on the Sabbath: to give life and to render judgment (5:21-23); C—Acceptance or rejection of Jesus' word is the criterion for the judgment that has already been anticipated (5:24); C1—The same criterion applies to those already physically dead, and they will eventually return to life as in Dan 12:2 (5:25); B1—Life and judgment are the prerogatives of the Son of Man (5:26-27); A1—The "greater works" promised in 5:20 are resurrection of the dead, judgment, and reward of the just and punishment of the wicked (5:28-29). The discourse ends as it began—an assertion of the Son's perfect unity with the one who sent him (5:30).

As Son of God, Jesus must work on the Sabbath to give life and judgment. Just as the Ancient of Days handed over these tasks to the Son of Man in Daniel 7, so the Father has handed them over to Jesus as his Son. The text also shows the tension between the "already" (5:20-24) and the "not yet" (5:25-29). The two dimensions are set side by side.

Having made claims about his authority as Son of God, Jesus must now explain the reasons why his claims should be accepted (5:31-47). First, he lists various witnesses to him (5:31-40), and then he criticizes the unbelief of his opponents (5:41-47).

So extraordinary is Jesus' claim to act as God does on the Sabbath that he needs witnesses to testify to the truth of his statements. His ultimate and most persuasive witness is the Father (5:32, 37-38). The "another who testifies" (5:32) is the

Father. The other witnesses are John the Baptist (5:33-35), the works that Jesus did (5:36), the Father (5:37-38), and the Scriptures (5:39-40).

The opponents already know the witness of John the Baptist (5:33-35), since their own emissaries had received his witness (1:19-28; 3:25-30). The description of John as "a burning and shining lamp" (5:35) may allude to Ps 132:17 ("I will place a lamp for my anointed"). But it does sound odd in view of the emphasis in 1:8: "He was not the light, but came to testify to the light." John's mission and popularity were temporary ("for a while," 5:35).

The second witness (5:36) is the "works" or signs that Jesus did (2:1-12; 4:46-54; 5:1-9). These actions point to Jesus' mission from the Father. The witness of the Father (5:37-38) has escaped Jesus' opponents because they failed to believe in him as the revealer of the Father. Likewise, the witness of Scripture (5:39) is ignored. Despite this array of witnesses, the opponents remain unwilling to believe. Their unbelief is attributed to a failure of will in 5:40 ("you do not want to come to me"). Instead of searching for eternal life through the Scriptures, they ought to turn to God's Son who alone can grant eternal life.

Mention of the Scriptures as a witness to Jesus leads to a more direct attack on the opponents (5:41-47). Their refusal to accept Jesus is tied to their lack of love for God and their desire for human praise. The charge that they accept those who come in their own name (5:43) may allude to greater acceptance for messianic pretenders or famous teachers than for Jesus who came in his Father's name. Then, the text attacks the opponents on a sensitive issue: the Scriptures (5:45-47). Whereas they imagine an opposition between Moses and Jesus, the text affirms a continuity. Out of loyalty to Moses they refuse to accept Jesus. But rather than defending them, Moses will serve as their accuser.

The controversy about the Sabbath in John 5 would have been especially meaningful in the context of the quarrel between the Johannine community and its Jewish rivals. The text gives a defense of the free attitude of Jesus and his followers toward work on the Sabbath. It uses that practice as a starting point for confirming the very high claims made about Jesus as Son of Man and Son of God. And it produces a list of witnesses that the opponents should have heeded. If (as seems likely) the opponents were emphasizing the Law of Moses and the Scriptures, the Christian claim that Moses was a witness to Jesus would have been especially daring.

Feeding of the Five Thousand (6:1-15)

Jesus' feeding of five thousand people (6:1-15) sets the stage for the so-called bread of life discourse (6:26-71). It is followed by the episode of Jesus walking on the water (6:16-25). The sequence of events is generally the same as in Mark 6: miraculous feeding (Mark 6:32-44) and walking on water (Mark 6:45-52). Some scholars argue that John 6 once preceded John 5, since the sequence of places (Galilee in chapter 4, Jerusalem in chapter 5, Galilee in chapter 6) is awkward.

The feeding of five thousand people is narrated in all the Gospels (Mark 6:32-44; Matt 14:13-21; Luke 9:10-17; John 6:1-15). The relation between the Synoptic and Johannine accounts is not entirely clear. All the accounts agree on the numbers: five thousand men, two hundred denarii worth of bread, five loaves and two fishes, and twelve baskets of fragments. For the feeding of four thousand people, see Mark 8:1-10; Matt 15:32-39. But there are enough differences to caution against concluding that John copied from one of the other accounts or put his story together from parts of others.

The feeding takes place near the Sea of Galilee, also called the Sea of Tiberias after the recently built city of Tiberias on its western shore (6:1). Only John attributes the crowd's interest to the signs that Jesus had done (6:2), and locates the event at Passover (6:4), thus preparing for the manna theme in the bread-of-life discourse. John's portrayal of Philip as spokesman for the disciples (6:5-7) and his note that a boy was the source of the five loaves and two fishes (6:8-9) are also unique.

The designation of the loaves as "barley" (6:9, 13) evokes the miraculous feeding of one hundred people by the prophet Elisha (2 Kings 4:42-44) and prepares for the crowd's designation of Jesus as the Prophet (6:14). John also brings out the eucharistic dimensions of the incident in 6:11-12: "Jesus took the loaves, gave thanks, and distributed them..."

A biblical model for Jesus' action in feeding a crowd appears in 2 Kings 4:42-44:

> A man came from Baal-shalishah bringing the man of God twenty barley loaves made from the first fruits, and fresh grain in the ear. "Give it to the people to eat," Elisha said. But his servant objected, "How can I set this before a hundred men?" "Give it to the people to eat," Elisha insisted. "For thus says the Lord, 'They shall eat and there shall be some left over.'" And when they had eaten, there was some left over, as the Lord had said.

The multiplication of the loaves and fishes is the fourth sign (6:14) done by Jesus (see 2:1-12; 4:46-54; 5:1-10). It contributes to our appreciation of Jesus' identity as the new Elisha, the prophet like Moses, and the king (6:15). It also sets the stage for the bread-of-life discourse. While not explicitly concerned with the Eucharist, the incident provides a broad context for appreciating Jesus as the bread of life.

The Walking on Water (6:16-25)

Jesus' fifth sign, his walking on the water (6:16-21), also appears in Mark 6:45-52 and Matt 14:22-33. In all these stories, Jesus' disciples find themselves rowing against a heavy wind in the middle of the Sea of Galilee. Then they see Jesus walking on the waters. He calms their fear by saying: "It is I. Do not be afraid" (John 6:20; Mark 6:50; Matt 14:27). In John the disciples travel from the eastern shore of the Sea of Galilee to the western shore where Capernaum is (6:17, 21; see 6:59).

In the Johannine setting, Jesus' statement "It is I" (6:20) is especially significant. In Exod 3:14 and Isaiah 41 and 43, God uses this formula to reveal himself. In this episode, Jesus is doing what the Bible says that only God can do: "He alone... treads upon the crests of the sea" (Job 9:8). Elsewhere in the

Fourth Gospel, Jesus uses the formula in reference to himself (see John 4:26; 8:24, 28, 58; 13:19; 18:5, 6, 8). Thus the Jews' charge ("making himself equal to God," 5:18) is ironically correct.

The crowd's puzzlement (6:22-25) confirms that Jesus had not set out with the disciples and prepares for the bread-of-life discourse at Capernaum.

Bread of Life Discourse (6:26-71)

The bread of life discourse (6:26-71) is loosely related to Jesus' feeding of the five thousand (6:1-15). The one who fed the large crowd now identifies himself as the bread of life. After introducing the basic themes (6:26-31), Jesus explains what the Father and he have done and how their work of salvation can be appropriated (6:32-58). The chapter concludes by reflecting on the varied reactions to Jesus' discourse (6:59-71).

There is a longstanding debate about the extent to which Jesus' discourse should be interpreted with reference to the Eucharist. The end of the discourse (6:51-58) is vividly eucharistic in its language. But how eucharistic is the language of 6:26-50? There the bread of life is Jesus himself and the revelation that he gives. Although there may be eucharistic overtones, the primary referent is Jesus the Wisdom of God. The vivid eucharistic language of 6:51-58 then places the whole discourse in a eucharistic key. In reading the discourse, it is best to follow the progress of the text and not to think eucharistically too early. There are many parallels with John 4 in which Jesus identifies himself and his teaching with the living water and the true food.

By way of introduction (6:26-31), Jesus ignores the crowd's foolish question ("Rabbi, when did you get here?" 6:25) and criticizes their failure even to grasp the meaning of the signs done by Jesus (6:26). He contrasts the food that perishes and the food that abides forever—that given by the Son of Man and certified by the Father (6:27). When the crowd questions Jesus about the "works of God," Jesus defines the "work of

God" as believing in him as the one sent by God (6:29).

The crowd in turn ignores Jesus' answer and wants to know what sign/work that Jesus is going to do (6:30). Without waiting for a response, they refer to ancient Israel eating manna in the wilderness (Exodus 16) and quote a biblical text ("He gave them bread from heaven to eat") that is very close to Psalm 78:24 (see Exod 16:4-5; Num 11:7-9). The thrust of Jesus' interpretation of this text will be to show that the subject of the verb is not Moses but "*my* Father" (6:32).

Thus the introduction has set up the dynamic of misunderstanding between Jesus and the questioners. It has also arrived at the basic topic: Who/what is the "bread of life," and how should one respond to him?

The body of the discourse (6:32-58) is built up according to a threefold, repeated pattern: (1) God's or Jesus' saving action on behalf of the world (6:32-33, 37-40, 48-51); (2) the audience's misunderstanding or rejection (6:34, 41-42, 52); and (3) what one must do to appropriate this salvation (6:35-36, 43-47, 53-58).

The first cycle in the pattern (6:32-36) emphasizes God's initiative. Jesus insists that God, rather than Moses, gave the bread mentioned in Psalm 78, and suggests that he himself is "the bread of God" that comes down from heaven and gives life to the world (6:32-33). When the audience asks for this bread always (6:34; see 4:15), Jesus states "I am the bread of life" and invites them to come to him and to believe in him (6:35-36).

The second cycle (6:37-47) stresses the historical action of Jesus. Sent by the Father and in perfect harmony with God's will, Jesus works to save all that the Father has given over to him. The salvation brought by Jesus involves both the eternal life begun through faith in him and Jesus' role in the resurrection (6:39-40). The audience, now identified as the "Jews" (6:41), misunderstands Jesus' true origin: Whereas they think of him only as the son of Joseph and Mary, Jesus is actually the one who came down from heaven. Their objection is described as "murmuring" (6:41, 43, 61)—the term used in Exodus 16 to refer to ancient Israel's negative reaction to Moses and the manna in the wilderness. In response (6:43-47)

Jesus insists that he is from God and has seen the Father (6:46). He also states that God takes the initiative in leading people to Jesus and thus to the Father: "No one can come to me unless the Father who sent me draw him" (6:44). For this statement, he appeals as scriptural proof to Isa 54:13 ("They shall all be taught by God"), thus implying that the "Jews" are not taught by God.

The third cycle (6:48-58) focuses on Jesus' sacrifice of himself. After identifying himself as the bread of life (6:48), Jesus contrasts the manna eaten in the wilderness and the bread from heaven that gives eternal life (6:49-51). Then he relates this bread to his own sacrificial death ("my flesh for the life of the world," 6:51) and thus prepares for the eucharistic development in 6:53-58. After the objection from the "Jews" in 6:52 ("How can this man give us his flesh to eat?"), Jesus insists on the necessity of eating his flesh and drinking his blood. The Semitic idiom "flesh and blood" is a way of describing the whole person. The word for "eat" in this context is very graphic: It means to crunch, gnaw, chew, etc. This shockingly realistic language indicates that one can appropriate Jesus' saving action by sharing in the Eucharist. The text also continues the combination of having eternal life in the present and being raised up on the last day (6:54). Sharing in Jesus' flesh and blood means "abiding" in him (6:56) and participating in the divine life that lasts forever (6:57-58).

In describing the varied reactions to Jesus' shocking claims, John distinguishes between the many disciples who now leave Jesus (6:60-66) and the Twelve who remain with him (6:67-71). He emphasizes Jesus' foreknowledge regarding the murmuring of his own disciples (6:61) and their rejection of him (6:64) as well as Judas' betrayal of him (6:64, 70-71). Peter here speaks the language of the Johannine community: "You have the words of eternal life. We have come to believe and are convinced (=have come to know) that you are the Holy One of God" (6:68-69).

Jesus at Tabernacles (7:1-52)

Along with Passover and Weeks (Pentecost), Tabernacles

was one of the three major Jewish feasts in which pilgrims came to Jerusalem. It was a harvest festival, celebrated for eight days in the fall (late September or early October). Its most distinctive feature was dwelling in booths or huts constructed of branches (see Lev 23:42-43). Though originally used as shelters for the harvesters, the booths or "tabernacles" (*sûkkôt* in Hebrew) were given a historical connection with Israel's exodus from Egypt: "When I led the Israelites out of the land of Egypt, I made them dwell in booths" (Lev 23:43).

The regulations for observing the feast of "Tabernacles" or "Booths" appear in Leviticus 23:33-36, 39-43:

> The Lord said to Moses, "Tell the Israelites: The fifteenth day of this seventh month is the Lord's feast of Booths, which shall continue for seven days.
>
> On the first day there shall be a sacred assembly, and you shall do no sort of work. For seven days you shall offer an oblation to the Lord, and on the eighth day you shall again hold a sacred assembly and offer an oblation to the Lord. On that solemn closing you shall do no sort of work.
>
> On the fifteenth day, then, of the seventh month, when you have gathered in the produce of the land, you shall celebrate a pilgrim feast of the Lord for a whole week. The first and the eighth day shall be days of complete rest.
>
> On the first day you shall gather foliage from majestic trees, branches of palms and boughs of myrtles and of valley poplars, and then for a week you shall make merry before the Lord, your God.
>
> By perpetual statute for you and your descendants you shall keep this pilgrim feast of the Lord for one whole week in the seventh month of the year. During this week every native Israelite among you shall dwell in booths, that your descendants may realize that, when I led the Israelites out of the land of Egypt, I made them dwell in booths. I, the Lord am your God."

Using the feast of Tabernacles as the focal point, one can make the following outline of the rest of the material: before Tabernacles (7:1-13), in the middle of Tabernacles (7:14-36), and on the last day of the feast (7:37-52). Much of the material takes the form of dialogues where the "Jews" misunderstand Jesus and so give him the opportunity and necessity to explain himself. The major themes are where Jesus came from (God) and where he is going (back to God).

Before Tabernacles (7:1-13). The scene before the feast takes place in Galilee (7:1, 9). Jesus' reluctance to go to Jerusalem in Judea stems from the desire of the "Jews" to kill him—a motif first raised in John 5:18 and expressed several times in John 7. Nevertheless, Jerusalem for John is Jesus' true home (see 4:44), and Jesus' presence at one of the great pilgrimage festivals is to be expected. The problem is one of timing.

The members of Jesus' family ("his brothers," 7:3) urge him to go up to Jerusalem and do signs. Up to this point, the healing of the lame man at Bethesda (5:1-16) on the Sabbath had taken place in Jerusalem. There were also allusions to other Judean signs in John 2:23; 3:2; 4:45. A pilgrimage feast like Tabernacles when so many Jews from the land of Israel and the Diaspora would be present was the perfect opportunity for Jesus to "manifest yourself to the world" (7:4). The evangelist adds parenthetically that Jesus' "brothers" did not believe in him (7:5). Whether these "brothers" were Jesus' cousins, or half-brothers (from Joseph's earlier marriage), or blood-brothers remains a matter of controversy (see Mark 6:3; Matt 13:55).

Jesus' response to his brothers' request (7:6-8) is similar to his answer to his mother at Cana (2:4). He says: "My time is not yet here. . . my time has not yet been fulfilled" (7:6, 8). Whereas the brothers view Tabernacles as the right time for Jesus to make a public display, the right time for Jesus' death, resurrection, and exaltation is Passover of the following spring (11:55). There are other ironies in Jesus' reply. When the brothers in 7:4 urge Jesus to manifest himself to "the world" (understood in a neutral sense as the general public), Jesus in 7:7 uses "world" in a negative sense to refer to those evil forces arrayed against him and hostile to him. In 7:8 he contrasts the brothers' going up to the feast as pilgrims with his own "going up" (exaltation) to the Father that will take place at Passover.

Jesus does eventually go up to the holy city, but in his own way ("not openly but in secret," 7:10) and not in response to his brothers' plans for him. The "Jews" (7:11, 13) are Jesus' opponents. But popular opinion is divided between those who regard Jesus as good and those who regard him as a deceiver (7:12). The "Jews" do not represent the entire Jewish people; they seem instead to be a powerful group within the people.

In the Middle of Tabernacles (7:14-36). Since Tabernacles lasted eight days (see Lev 23:36, 39), the middle of the feast would be the fourth or fifth day. This provides the occasion for Jesus to enter into dialogue with the "Jews" about where he got his learning (7:15-24), where he came from (7:25-31), and where he is going (7:32-36).

The "Jews" first want to know where Jesus got his learning (7:15-24): "How does he know Scripture without having studied?" Their question presumes that Jesus had not studied under a distinguished teacher and that he did not teach in the usual ways (see Mark 1:22: "He taught them as one having authority and not as the scribes"). In response, Jesus denies that he is self-taught or speaks on his own. Rather, his teacher is the one who sent him—God the Father (7:16). Those who seek God's will know that (7:17)—an oblique criticism of his opponents. The goal of Jesus' teaching is God's glory, not his own (7:18). So Jesus' teacher is God, and the goal of his teaching is God's glory.

Debate about the source of Jesus' knowledge of Scripture leads to an illustration of that knowledge in 7:19-24. The passage takes up the healing on the Sabbath described in John 5:1-16: "I performed one work and all of you are amazed" (7:21). Jesus first accuses his opponents of not keeping the law of Moses—probably because they are seeking to kill him (5:18), an innocent man. Their denial (7:20) highlights the irony that, in fact, they are trying to kill him. Jesus' defense (7:22-23) takes the form of a scriptural argument. According to Scripture (Gen 17:12; Lev 12:3), a male child was to be circumcised on the eighth day after his birth. If the boy was born on a Sabbath, he was to be circumcised on the following Sabbath. Thus circumcision overrides the Sabbath rest. From this scriptural premise, Jesus argues that, if what pertains to one part of the body can be done on the Sabbath, what pertains to the health of the whole person (as in 5:1-16) can surely be carried out. This reasoning is characterized as "judging justly" (7:24).

Then, some of the people of Jerusalem raise the question about where Jesus came from (7:25-31). They admit that some seek to kill Jesus (7:25; see 7:20). They, however, are impressed with Jesus and wonder whether the authorities have realized that Jesus is the Messiah (7:26). Their objection to Jesus is that they know where he is from—from Nazareth. They hold a tradition about the hidden Messiah (7:27). Since they know that Jesus came from Nazareth, it is clear that he could not be the Messiah.

The people's misunderstanding about Jesus and his origin provides the occasion for Jesus to announce in 7:28-29 that he is really from God: "I am from him, and he sent me" (7:29). Again, the popular response is divided between those who are impressed by Jesus' signs (7:31) and those who want to arrest him (7:30). But nothing really happens "because his hour had not yet come" (7:30).

Finally, the "Jews" want to know where Jesus is going (7:32-36). The unlikely coalition of Pharisees and chief priests (probably Sadducees) seeks to arrest Jesus, who announces: "I will be with you only a little while longer, and then I will go to the one who sent me. You will look for me but not find me, and where I am you cannot come" (7:33-34). Of course, Jesus speaks of his exaltation and return to the Father. But the "Jews" are totally puzzled and misunderstand him. They think that he might be going to the Diaspora to teach non-Jews there. The irony is that, when John's Gospel was written and first read, Gentiles outside of the land of Israel were being taught about Jesus. And Jesus himself had returned to his heavenly Father and so was in a far better place than the Diaspora.

On the Last Day of the Feast (7:37-52). The biblical instruction about the feast of Booths or Tabernacles gives special prominence to the last day: "On the eighth day you shall again hold a sacred assembly and offer an oblation to the Lord. On that solemn closing you shall do no sort of work" (Lev 23:36; see 23:39). On "the last and greatest day of the feast" (John 7:37), Jesus makes a public proclamation (7:37b-38), which generates varied reactions among the people (7:40-44) and even more negative response among the leaders (7:45-52).

Tabernacles takes place in the fall of the year, at the beginning of the rainy season, after some six months of dry weather. According to Mishnah *Sukkah* 4:9, one of the ceremonies associated with Tabernacles consisted in filling a flagon full of water from the pool at Siloam (see John 9:7, 11), bringing it through the "Water Gate," and taking it to the temple area. So when Jesus proclaims in 7:37, "Let anyone who thirsts come to me and drink," he is playing on a major motif of the feast. The precise origin of the Scripture quotation in 7:38 ("Rivers of living water will flow from within him") is uncertain. Some find a Moses-background (Exod 17:6; Num 20:11), and others point to Ezek 47:1-11 or Isa 55:1-3a. Likewise, the referent of "within him" is disputed with some arguing for the believer (on grammatical grounds) and others arguing for Jesus (on theological grounds). The Evangelist's comment in 7:39 connects the "living water" (see John 4:10, 11, 14; 19:34) with the gift of the Spirit after Jesus' death and resurrection (see John 20:22).

Some in the crowd identify Jesus as "the prophet" (Deut 18:15, 18). Others confess him to be "the Messiah," which generates a debate about the Messiah's origin (7:41-43). Since the Messiah is to come from Bethlehem of Judah (Mic 5:1, 3; see Matt 2:6; Luke 2:4, 11, 15) and since "everybody knew" that Jesus came from Galilee, therefore he could not be the Messiah. Of course, the primary Johannine irony is that Jesus came from his heavenly Father. There may also be in the background the Synoptic Gospel tradition that Jesus was born in Bethlehem.

The chapter concludes with a rejection of the claims about Jesus by the chief priests and Pharisees (7:45). They accuse the guards sent out by them to seize Jesus (7:32) of having been deceived by him (7:12) and dismiss the popular enthusiasm for him as the product of the crowd's ignorance of the law (7:49). They dismiss Nicodemus' appeal for due process (7:52) as a "Galilean" idea and assert that prophets (or the prophet of Deut 18:15, 18) do not come from Galilee.

The Woman Taken in Adultery (7:53-8:11)

Although this text may contain an early story connected with Jesus, it is generally conceded that it was not originally part of John's Gospel. Its style, vocabulary, and theology are quite different from what one usually finds in the Fourth Gospel. It is absent from the earliest and best manuscripts. In some manuscripts, it appears after John 7:36, or at the end of John's Gospel as a kind of appendix, or after Luke 21:38. In fact, the story is more Lukan than Johannine in almost every respect.

How did it get to be part of the text of John's Gospel? Some view it as an illustration of Jesus' saying in John 8:15 ("You judge by appearances, but I do not judge anyone") or 8:46a ("Can any of you charge me with sin?"). Others connect it with the activity of Jesus the prophet like Moses of Deut 18:15, 18 (see 7:40, 52). Despite its varied textual history, the episode is considered part of the church's Scripture today.

The setting (7:53-8:2) is the Jerusalem temple area—associated in the other Gospels with passion week. There Jesus is teaching the people. A confrontation (8:3-6a) occurs when the scribes and Pharisees bring before Jesus a woman caught in the act of adultery. According to Lev 20:10 and Deut 22:22-24, the penalty for adultery was supposed to be death, though it is doubtful that such punishment was actually carried out in Jesus' day. Stoning was the mode of capital punishment (Deut 22:24), and the first stones were to be thrown by the witnesses (Deut 17:7). The aim was to "test" Jesus (8:6a): Would he be faithful to the letter of the Mosaic law (even if this procedure were not being carried out), or would he disregard the law in favor of his well-known gospel of mercy?

Instead of ruling directly on the case, Jesus begins to write on the ground with his finger. What he wrote (the sins of the accusers, a biblical quotation, etc.) is a matter of speculation. But Jesus' challenge to the accusers in 8:7 ("Let the one among you who is without sin be the first to throw a stone at her") probably reflects the rule in Deut 19:15-21 that the accusers be just themselves. Jesus knows beforehand that they cannot meet this test.

As the accusers disappear and the woman is left alone with Jesus (8:8-11), Jesus shows compassion toward the sinner while urging her to sin no more. He forgives the sinner without condoning the sin, thus preserving the delicate balance between justice and mercy that is characteristic of the biblical tradition.

Light of the World (8:12-20)

It is not certain that we are to assume a setting at the celebration of Tabernacles for chapter 8. If we do so assume, then Jesus' proclamation of himself as "light of the world" (8:12) takes on added significance. According to Mishnah *Sukkah* 5:2-4 at Tabernacles, four golden candlesticks were lighted in the Court of Women at the Jerusalem temple, where the treasury (8:20) was and where Jesus was speaking. As in the case of 7:37-38 where Jesus alludes to the water-rituals at Tabernacles, so here he may be playing off his own claim to be light of the world against the background of the light ceremonies held in the very place in which he was speaking.

The real topic of the passage, however, is not the content of Jesus' claim, but rather the propriety of his bearing witness to himself. The same topic was treated at length in John 5:31-47 where various witnesses to Jesus (John the Baptist, Jesus' works, the Scriptures, his heavenly Father) were summoned to confirm his testimony about himself. Here in 8:13-20 when the Pharisees deny the validity of Jesus' claims about himself, they object on the grounds that Jesus' testimony cannot be verified (8:13). The thrust of Jesus' response is that his heavenly Father stands behind his testimony. He first appeals to his heavenly origin and destiny (8:14) and asserts that both he and his Father witness to him (8:16, 18). In the background is the biblical tradition of needing the testimony of two or three witnesses to establish a judicial fact (Deut 17:6; 19:15; Num 35:30), especially in a capital case (8:17). When the opponents want to know where Jesus' Father is (8:19), Jesus asserts that they know neither him nor his Father. This assertion then prepares for what can be called a summary of the entire Gospel: "If you knew me, you would know my Father also" (8:19).

Underlying the argument about the validity of Jesus' claims about himself is the pattern of dualism described in John 3. Those who follow Jesus have the light of the world, whereas those who do not walk in darkness (8:12). Jesus knows who he is and what the law teaches; his opponents do not know him, the law, or his Father. They judge according to the "flesh" ("by appearances") in 8:15.

Statements, Misunderstandings, Corrections (8:21-59)

The dialogue form becomes even stronger in the rest of chapter 8. In eight short segments (8:21-24a, 24b-29, 30-36, 37-40, 41-46, 47-50, 51-55, 56-58), there is a statement by Jesus, a misunderstanding by his audience (usually the "Jews"), and a correction and further explanation from Jesus. The opponents function as literary foils to allow greater clarity on Jesus' part. The items under discussion may reflect the struggles between the Johannine community and the synagogue toward the end of the first century. The chief topics are the identity of Jesus and the rejection of Jesus by some of his own people.

In the first segment (8:21-24a), Jesus announces that he is going away (to the Father) and his opponents cannot come but will die in their sin (of unbelief). They assume that he is talking about suicide (but in fact they will be responsible for his death). Jesus goes on to explain the gulf that separates him from them in terms of dualism: They are from below and belong to "this world," but he is from above and does not belong to this world. Being from below and belonging to this world puts the opponents within the sphere of sin and thus subject to the power of death.

In the second segment (8:24b-29), Jesus warns: "For if you do not believe that I AM, you will die in your sins." By using the expression "I AM," Jesus applies to himself a title used of God in the Hebrew Bible (Isa 43:10-12; see Exod 3:14; Deut 32:39; John 4:26; 6:20; 13:19; 18:5, 6, 8). But the opponents misunderstand and ask Jesus to finish his sentence ("Who are you?"). Jesus goes on to explain that his divine status will become clear only when he as Son of Man is lifted up (a play on Jesus' crucifixion as a key step in his exaltation). Moreover, Jesus' divine status is never independent of the Father, who sent him and is the source and goal of Jesus' activity.

The third segment (8:30-36) revolves around the theme of freedom. When Jesus promises knowledge of the truth and freedom to those who abide in his word, the "Jews" object that, as sons of Abraham, they had never been slaves. Whereas they take freedom in a political sense, Jesus introduces the idea of spiritual freedom and spiritual slavery (to sin): "Everyone who commits sin is a slave of sin" (8:34). He claims that only the Son can free people from sin by appealing to the process by which slaves in a household gain their freedom (that is, by the mediation of a son).

The fourth segment (8:37-40) concerns what it means to be Abraham's children. When the opponents claim Abraham as their father (8:39), Jesus insists that Abraham's children must do Abraham's works. Since Jesus is revealing God and the opponents are trying to kill Jesus, the implication is that they are not behaving as Abraham's children should and therefore forfeit their identity. For a similar argument, see Paul's letter to the Galatians, especially chapter 3.

In the fifth segment (8:41-46), the opponents claim God as their Father. Jesus denies their claim on the ground that they reject him, whom God has sent (8:42-43). Since God is not their father, it must be the devil ("You belong to your father the devil"), because they do his works (murder, lies). In these charges there may be allusions to the devil as the one ultimately responsible for Cain's murder of Abel (Gen 4:1-16) and the serpent's deception of Eve (Gen 3:1-7).

When in the sixth segment (8:47-50) Jesus concludes that the opponents do not belong to God because they do not listen to God's words (from him), the "Jews" accuse him of being a Samaritan (a heretic) and possessed (by a demon). Jesus denies their charges and reaffirms his dedication to seeking God's glory.

The seventh segment (8:51-55) takes as its starting point Jesus' promise of eternal life to those who keep his words. The opponents counter with the fact that Abraham and the prophets died, and ask who Jesus thinks that he is. Jesus responds by emphasizing his closeness to the Father: "I know him and I keep his word."

The eighth and final segment (8:56-58) deals with the relationship between Jesus and Abraham. When Jesus claims Abraham's approval (8:56), the "Jews" deny that he could have any relationship to Abraham since he was under fifty years of age (see Luke 3:23). In reply Jesus again uses the divine epithet: "Before Abraham came to be, I AM." Regarding such a claim to be blasphemy (see Lev 24:16), the opponents try to stone Jesus.

From these debates, the opponents (the "Jews") emerge as belonging to the wrong side—the side of the devil, this world, sin, death, ignorance, etc. Jesus emerges as God's Son and messenger, the Son of Man who will be exalted, the one who can be called by the divine epithet "I AM." He can give freedom from sin, identity as Abraham's offspring, and eternal life.

The Man Born Blind (9:1-41)

The story of Jesus healing a man born blind (9:1-41) is a self-contained unit. After the account of the healing (9:1-7), there is a series of encounters that serve to specify the significance of what happened and the identity of the healer: between the neighbors and the man (9:8-12), between the Pharisees and the man (9:13-17), between the "Jews" and the man's parents (9:18-23), between the "Jews" and the man (9:24-34), between Jesus and the man (9:35-39), and between the Pharisees and Jews (9:40-41). As the sixth sign in the Gospel (see 2:1-12; 4:46-54, 5:1-9; 6:1-15; 6:16-21), this healing leads to reflection on Jesus as the "light of the world" (9:5; see 8:12).

The references to expulsion from the synagogue (9:22, 34-35) suggest that the story and the accompanying dialogues had particular significance for the Johannine community. After A.D. 70 with the loss of the Jerusalem temple and political control over the land of Israel, the Johannine community and the "Jews" were rivals in their claims to continue the Jewish heritage. The story of the man born blind should be read at two levels: the time of Jesus' earthly ministry (ca. A.D. 30), and the time of the Johannine community's struggle with the "Jews" (ca. A.D. 90). It tells us some of the issues that divided the two movements and how those issues affected the lives of Jews in the first century. It gives particular attention to the theme of growth in spiritual insight: The man born blind grows in his ability to recognize who Jesus is, while the Pharisees/"Jews" become ever blinder. The religious leaders who should see reject the light, and the man born blind receives the light and sees physically and spiritually.

The account of the healing of the man born blind (9:1-7)

provides the occasion for the various encounters. It consists of a narrative (9:1, 6-7) and a conversation (9:2-5). The narrative section tells about the man's condition ("blind from birth") and how Jesus tested his faith by putting him through a healing ritual (see Mark 7:33; 8:23) involving a paste made out of spittle and soil. The instruction to wash in the pool of Siloam (south of the temple area) is reminiscent of the prophet Elisha's command to Naaman the Syrian (2 Kings 5:10-14) to wash in the Jordan River. The conversation (9:2-5) begins when Jesus' disciples inquire as to who sinned—the man or his parents— that he should be born blind. Jesus sets aside the broad theological question (see Exod 20:5 and Ezek 18:20 for op- posing viewpoints) and contends that this particular case of physical blindness had a providential purpose in making manifest the works of God. Jesus does the works of the one who sent him (9:4); he is the "one sent" ("Siloam," 9:7). The reason for healing on the Sabbath (9:14) is given here: The present time is "day," and the "light" of the world must work while he is in the world (9:4-5). During the passion ("night") Jesus will not be able to do such things.

The first encounter (9:8-12) involves the man and his neighbors. It serves to establish the reality of the cure: Those who knew the man previously as a blind beggar (see Mark 10:46-52) testify that now he sees. The dispute among the neighbors and acquaintances is resolved by the man's admis- sion that he is the one who was healed (9:9). When asked how he was healed, the man provides a factual summary: "The man called Jesus made clay. . . " (9:11). He knows that Jesus healed him but does not know his whereabouts (9:12). As the encounters proceed, the man born blind will grow in insight regarding the true identity of "the man called Jesus."

The second encounter (9:13-17) is between the "Pharisees" and the man born blind. In the late first century, the move- ment led by the Pharisees seems to have been the chief rival of the Johannine community. Here the term "Pharisees" is inter- changeable with the "Jews" (9:18). Only in 9:14 are we told that the healing took place on a Sabbath (see John 5:9-18; 7:20-24). Since the man had been born blind and his condition was not life-threatening, Jesus could have waited until the

Sabbath was over. Furthermore, Jesus' action in making the paste out of spittle and dirt could be construed as work forbidden on the Sabbath. Jesus has already given his defense: As light of the world, he must work while it is day (9:4-5). Jesus' apparent carelessness about work on the Sabbath leads to a debate among the Pharisees. Some claim that Jesus could not be from God because he leads people astray by not keeping the Sabbath (Deut 13:1-5), and others argue that only a good person could perform such signs (9:16). At this point, the Pharisees have still not made up their minds about Jesus. The man born blind, however, is growing in his appreciation of Jesus. Now he says that Jesus is "a prophet" (9:17), presumably because he can perform signs as Elijah and Elisha did.

The third encounter (9:18-23) is between the "Jews" and the parents of the man born blind. The "Jews" want greater certainty about the reality of the cure. The parents are willing only to testify that he is their son and that he was born blind. For further information about the healing and the healer, the "Jews" will have to question the man himself (9:20-21, 23). The Evangelist explains the parents' reticence as due to "fear of the 'Jews'" (see 7:13; 19:38; 20:19). He adds that the "Jews" had decided that whoever confessed Jesus as the Messiah would be put "out of the synagogue" (*aposynagōgos,* see 12:42; 16:2). This explanation probably alludes to the fact that around A.D. 90, Jewish Christians, who openly confessed Jesus as the Messiah, were being excluded from the Jewish synagogues. The reticence of the man's parents is symbolic of those who found themselves "sitting on the fence" and unwilling to make the break with the synagogue.

The fourth encounter (9:24-34) is between the "Jews" and the man born blind. It revolves around the assertion "we know" (9:24, 29, 31). The Jews claim that "we know" that Jesus is a sinner (9:24); the man replies that all he knows is that he was blind but now he sees (9:25). When the "Jews" inquire again about the healing (9:26), the man naively suggests that perhaps they wish to become Jesus' disciples, too (9:27). This suggestion infuriates the "Jews" who claim to be Moses' disciples: "We know that God spoke to Moses, but we do not know where this one is from" (9:29). Those who ought to know that Jesus is "from above" do not know where he is from. Their claim to be Moses' disciples as opposed to Jesus' disciples (9:28) may reflect rival claims in the synagogue-church struggle of the late first century. In response, the man born blind adopts the rhetorical style of the "Jews": "We know that God does not listen to sinners..." (9:31). Therefore, Jesus must be "from God" (9:33). His belief in Jesus is growing (from "the man called Jesus" to "a prophet" to the one "from God"), whereas the Pharisees/"Jews" have moved from confusion to the conviction that Jesus is a sinner. In reaction to the man's confession that Jesus is "from God", the "Jews" throw him out—perhaps another allusion to exclusion from the synagogue in the late first century (9:34; see 9:22).

5) The fifth encounter (9:35-39) is between Jesus and the man born blind. After the man's expulsion, Jesus seeks him out and leads him to an even more correct faith: He comes to believe in Jesus as the Son of Man (see John 1:51; 3:13, 14; 5:27; 6:27, 53, 62; 12:23; 13:31), addresses him as "Lord," and does him homage ("he worshiped him"). In 9:39 Jesus picks up on the Son of Man's role as judge and draws the basic lesson of the entire chapter: Those who do not see see, and those who do see become blind (9:39).

The final encounter (9:40-41) between the Pharisees and Jesus shows their spiritual blindness ("Surely we are not also blind, are we?"). Jesus not only acknowledges their blindness, but also counts it as "sin" precisely because they claim "We see."

In the story of the man born blind, we see on the one hand a steady growth in insight and faith, and on the other hand a decline in insight and faith. The man's parents represent those who try to remain neutral in the struggle. The Evangelist's sympathies are clearly with the man born blind and against the Pharisees/Jews. Beginning from the sign done by Jesus and proceeding through the six dialogues, the Evangelist has provided a picture of the struggle facing his community in the late first century. He has shown how the "blind" come to see who Jesus is and how those who think that they "see" and "know" are actually blind to the great spiritual realities around them.

The Good Shepherd (10:1-21)

The "good shepherd" discourse appears without a narrative setting and without any obvious connection to what precedes it. It consists of a parable (10:1-5) that elicits puzzlement (10:6) and an explanation of two features of the parable—the gate and the shepherd (10:7-18)—that elicits division among the "Jews" (10:19-21). The discourse emphasizes the relationship of intimacy between the shepherd and the sheep. It also points forward to Jesus' death as a voluntary sacrifice undertaken on behalf of his flock.

The setting of the parable is a "sheepfold"—a pen formed by stone walls with one gate for entry and exit (10:1). The parable contrasts the actions of "a thief and a robber" who enters anywhere but the proper place (10:1) and those of the shepherd who goes through the gate and is admitted by the gatekeeper (10:2-3a). Then the parable focuses on the intimate relationship between the shepherd and his sheep: "the sheep hear his voice, as he calls his own sheep by name and leads them out" (10:3b). Outside the sheepfold, the sheep follow the leadership of the shepherd "because they recognize his voice" (10:4) and do not follow a stranger "because they do not recognize the voice of strangers" (10:5). The reaction of the audience (who they are is not specified) is puzzlement: "They did not realize what he was trying to tell them" (10:6).

Taken by itself and without the explanations offered in 10:7-18, the "figure of speech" remains puzzling. In the Hebrew Bible, the image of shepherd is frequently applied to God: "The Lord is my shepherd" (Ps 23:1); "O shepherd of Israel, hearken, O guide of the flock of Joseph!" (Ps 80:1); "the God who has been my shepherd from my birth to this day" (Gen 48:15); "because of the Shepherd, the Rock of Israel" (Gen 49:24). The most extensive development of the "shepherd" image for God appears in Ezekiel 34: "I myself will look after and tend my sheep. As a shepherd tends his flock when he finds himself among his scattered sheep, so will I tend my sheep..." (34:11-12). In Ezek 34:23, God speaks of transferring his office to a Messiah figure: "I will appoint one shepherd over them, my servant David; he shall pasture them and be their shepherd."

Who is the shepherd of the parable? Is it God or Jesus? Of course, for John there is no sharp distinction since Jesus is the one sent by God to reveal the Father. Is the shepherd the God of Israel as in most of the biblical tradition? Or has the image been transferred to the Son of David? The same ambiguity appears in the "good shepherd" parables in Matt 18:10-14 and Luke 15:3-7, where Jesus' concern for the "lost" is based on and is a manifestation of God's care for such people.

The explanation (10:7-18) aims to clear up the confusion. Actually, there are two explanations. First, Jesus identifies himself as the gate (10:7-10), and then he identifies himself as the good shepherd (10:11-18).

As the gate for the sheep (10:7), Jesus provides the way by which people can be saved (10:9) and have life more abundantly (10:10). The identification of Jesus as the "gate" is surprising, since the focus of 10:1-5 was the shepherd. The "thieves and robbers" (10:8, 10; see 10:1) are identified as "all who came before me" (10:8). Since they can hardly be the great figures of the Hebrew Bible (Abraham, Moses, David, etc.), they must be the "Jews" or Pharisees, or the Jewish leaders, or (most likely) false messiahs to whom the sheep wisely did not listen. Nothing is said about the identity of the gatekeeper (10:3). Some interpreters find in 10:7-10 an allusion to the rivalry between the Johannine community and the "Jews" over what is the proper way of life in Israel now that the temple has been destroyed.

As the good shepherd (10:11-18), Jesus contrasts his behavior with that of the hired man (10:11-13). Whereas the hireling abandons the sheep at the sight of a wolf, the good shepherd is willing to risk his own life for the good of the sheep. No attempt is made to identify the hireling or the wolf, but again there may be an allusion to events in the history of the Johannine community.

The assertion that the good shepherd lays down his life for his sheep leads to a reflection on Jesus' death and resurrection (10:14-18). Jesus dies willingly for others ("I will lay down my life...I lay it down on my own") because he knows the Father and he knows his sheep (10:14-15). In a departure from the usual New Testament portrayal of Jesus' resurrection as something done to him ("he was raised"), Jesus affirms in 10:17-18 that "I lay down my life in order to take it up again...I have power to lay it down and power to take it up again."

The life of the Johannine community is a sub-theme of 10:14-18. The goal is "one flock, one shepherd" (10:16). There is also reference to "other sheep that do not belong to this fold" (10:16)—perhaps an allusion to Gentile believers seeking to be part of the Johannine community, or to a rival Jewish-Christian group.

Only when the speech is over do we learn that the audience was the "Jews" (10:19). Whereas in John 9, the "Jews" passed through a cycle of reactions to Jesus from division (9:16) to total spiritual blindness (9:39-41), here they are still at the stage of division again. Some say that Jesus is possessed and crazy and therefore not worth listening to (10:20). Others argue that a possessed person could not give sight to a blind man (10:21; see 9:16, 31-33).

There are many obscurities in the "good shepherd" discourse. The imagery is confusing; some figures are not explained at all; there are allusions to the history of the Johannine community that escape us now. But the basic point is clear: Jesus knows and loves his own—enough to lay down his life for them. He acts in accord with God's will and power ("This command I have received from my Father," 10:18). Hirelings, false shepherds, and pseudo-messiahs do not act as he does.

Jesus at Hanukkah (10:22-42)

The Jewish festival of Hanukkah (Dedication) celebrated the re-dedication of the Jerusalem temple in 164 B.C. under Judas Maccabeus (see 1 Macc 4:59). During the three preceding years, the Jerusalem temple had been used for rites foreign to the Jewish tradition. This innovation (perceived as sacrilege by some Jews) took place during the time of the Syrian emperor, Antiochus IV Epiphanes. After native Jewish resistance and the death of Antiochus IV, the traditional cult was restored under Judas. Hanukkah commemorates the restoration of the Jerusalem temple in 164 B.C. It occurs in late November or December ("It was winter," 10:22).

"Hanukkah" means dedication (of the temple). How it became an annual festival among Jews is described in 1 Maccabees 4:52-59:

> Early in the morning on the twenty-fifth day of the ninth month, that is, the month of Chislev, in the year one hundred and forty-eight, they arose and offered sacrifice according to the law on the new altar of holocausts that they had made. On the Anniversary of the day on which the Gentiles had defiled it, on that very day it was re-consecrated with songs, harps, flutes, and cymbals. All the people prostrated themselves and adored and praised Heaven, who had given them success.
>
> For eight days they celebrated the dedication of the altar and joyfully offered holocausts and sacrifices of deliverance and praise. They ornamented the facade of the temple with gold crowns and shields; they repaired the gates and the priests' chambers and furnished them with doors. There was great joy among the people now that the disgrace of the Gentiles was removed. Then Judas and his brothers and the entire congregation of Israel decreed that the days of the dedication of the altar should be observed with joy and gladness on the anniversary every year for eight days, from the twenty-fifth day of the month Chislev.

Jesus' Hanukkah dialogue is set in the Portico of Solomon (10:23), a colonnade on the east side of the temple enclosure, facing the Mount of Olives. The same place is mentioned in Acts 3:11 and 5:12; the latter text suggests that it became a gathering place for early Christians in Jerusalem.

The first part of the dialogue (10:24-31) concerns Jesus' identity as the Messiah: "If you are the Messiah, tell us plainly" (10:24). The questioners are the "Jews," and their questioning arises out of the division among them mentioned in 10:19. Jesus replies that he has already told them who he is and that his works done in God's name testify to his identity (10:25). Then reaching back to the "good shepherd" discourse, Jesus explains the "Jews'" lack of faith in him: "But you do not believe because you are not among my sheep" (10:26). This in turn leads to a summary of the "good shepherd" discourse (10:27) and an assertion that Jesus gives eternal life (10:28). The combination of Messiah and shepherd reminds the reader of David, the model for all Jewish concepts of Messiah; it perhaps alludes to Ezek 34:23: "I will appoint one shepherd over them to pasture them, my servant David; he shall pasture them and be their shepherd." Jesus bases his power to give "eternal life" to his sheep on his intimate relationship with God: "The Father and I are one" (10:30). The plural subject and verb coupled with the singular predicate ("one") were very important in the development of the doctrine of the Trinity. The response of the "Jews" to the first part of the dialogue is hostile: "The Jews again picked up rocks to stone him" (10:31).

The second part of the dialogue (10:32-39) revolves around the charge of blasphemy against Jesus: "You, a man, are making yourself God" (10:33). According to the "Jews," Jesus' claim to be one with the Father is the equivalent of blasphemy—for which the punishment was death by stoning (see Lev 24:16). In the other Gospels, the charge of blasphemy is raised only at Jesus' trial, shortly before his death (Mark 14:64; Matt 26:65). Jesus' answer to their charge takes the form of a scriptural argument. In Psalm 82 God addresses the members of the heavenly council. In Jesus' time these councilors were understood to be angels. In verse 6 God addresses them: "You are gods." Jesus' argument proceeds in typical Jewish fashion: If God calls angelic judges "gods" in Scripture, why is Jesus accused of blasphemy for calling himself "Son of God" (10:34-36)? The key word in Jesus' defense is "consecrated": "the one whom the Father has consecrated and sent into the world" (10:36). Hanukkah was the commemoration of the (re-)consecration of the Jerusalem temple, and so Jesus is being described with a term appropriate to the festival. Having made his scriptural argument, Jesus returns to the relation between faith and his works (10:37-38; see 10:25). The aim of his works is to encourage belief that "the Father is in me, and I am in the Father" (10:38). The reaction to the second part of the dialogue is also hostile (10:39): "They tried again to arrest him."

The hostility of the "Jews" leads Jesus to withdraw from Jerusalem and Judea to Transjordan. This action seems to mark the end of Jesus' public activity. But for the Lazarus episode in chapter 11 he will return to Judea, only to withdraw again at the end (see 11:54). The first withdrawal returns Jesus to where his public ministry began—in the circle of John the Baptist (see 1:28)—and reiterates John's testimony about Jesus. It also contrasts the unbelief that Jesus met among the "Jews" and the belief that he met elsewhere.

Jesus' Hanukkah dialogue contributes to the unfolding of his identity: He is Messiah-Shepherd and Son of God. It also illustrates again the implacable hostility of the "Jews," who try to stone him and to arrest him. Jesus is indeed a prophet without honor in his native place (4:44).

The Raising of Lazarus (11:1-44)

The story of Jesus raising Lazarus from the dead (11:1-44) is the longest episode in the Fourth Gospel. As the last "sign" during Jesus' public ministry (see 2:1-12; 4:46-54; 5:1-9; 6:1-15; 6:16-21; 9:1-7), it goes beyond all the others as a proof of Jesus' power. It signifies Jesus' ability to give life: "I am the resurrection and the life" (11:25). The irony is that Jesus' giving life back to Lazarus results in the plot to take his own life (11:45-57). Though there are loose connections with the episodes of the son of the widow of Nain (Luke 7:11-17) and Lazarus and the rich man (Luke 16:19-31; see also Luke 7:36-50; 10:38-42; 19:41-44), the raising of Lazarus appears only in John's Gospel.

Many outlines have been proposed for the Lazarus episode. The following outline places at the center the identification of Jesus as the resurrection and the life: A—introduction (11:1-6), B—the fact of Lazarus' death (11:7-17), C—the identification of Jesus (11:18-27), B1—the fact of Lazarus' death (11:28-37), and A1—conclusion (11:38-44). The major themes are life and death, faith, bringing to life again, love, and glory. The Lazarus story is the perfect preparation for the passion narrative, because it helps to explain the hostility of the Jewish leaders against Jesus and gives insight into the ultimate significance of Jesus' passion and death (triumph over death, glory for the Son, life for others).

The introduction (11:1-6) provides information about the characters and how they relate to one another. Lazarus from Bethany (near Jerusalem) was ill. He was the brother of Mary and Martha. None of these characters have been mentioned so far in the Gospel, though Mary and Martha are introduced as if we already knew them (11:1). Mary is further identified by referring to an episode that is recounted only in the next chapter (12:1-8). The description of Lazarus as "the one you love" (11:3) has led some to identify him as the "beloved disciple" and the author of the Gospel, but this is very speculative. Jesus in turn knows and loves all three of these characters (11:5). Besides introducing the main characters, the first segment also sets the scene for the miracle whereby Lazarus will be restored to life. Instead of reacting immediately to the news of Lazarus' illness, Jesus remains where he was for two more days (11:6). He delays not out of indifference toward his friend's illness but "for the glory of God, that the Son of God may be glorified through it" (11:4). The Johannine Jesus acts out of full knowledge of what is ahead of him.

The second segment (11:7-16) establishes Jesus' resolve to go up to Jerusalem and the fact of Lazarus' death by dialogues between Jesus and his disciples. In the first dialogue (11:7-10), Jesus makes a proposal: "Let us go back to Judea" (11:7). When the disciples object that the "Jews" want to kill him (11:8; see 8:59; 10:31, 39), Jesus answers with a somewhat mysterious saying to the effect that he must act promptly (11:9-10). His public ministry is still the time of the "light of the world"; he must act before the "night" of the passion (12:35; 13:30) closes in. The second dialogue (11:11-15) involves a misunderstanding on the disciples' part. When Jesus announces that Lazarus is "asleep" and that he is going to awaken him (11:11), the disciples assume that Lazarus is sleeping and will be alright (11:12). The irony is that they use the word that can also mean "he will be saved" and thus unwittingly move to the spiritual level on which Jesus is speaking. Then Jesus announces plainly that "Lazarus has died" (11:14) and that the purpose of all this is "that you may believe" (11:15). The proposal of Thomas: "Let us also go to die with him" (11:16) prepares for Jesus' passion and death that will come about as a consequence of the Lazarus episode. It also highlights with suitable irony the failure of Jesus' disciples to stand by Jesus during the passion (16:32).

The central segment (11:17-27) sets the scene at Bethany (11:17-20) and features the dialogue between Martha and Jesus (11:21-27). In Palestine at Jesus' time, burial took place on the day of death, and then the mourning period began. Since Jesus had delayed for two days (11:6) and since it took time to travel to Judea from across the Jordan (10:40), Jesus and his disciples arrived after the burial (see 11:39). Lazarus was really dead. Bethany was a small village, about two miles east of Jerusalem. The "Jews" in this episode are not hostile. Rather, they seek to console the sisters (11:19, 31, 33), and some even come to believe in Jesus (11:45).

The heart of the episode is the conversation between Martha and Jesus (11:21-27). Martha begins by affirming that, if Jesus had been there, Lazarus would not have died (11:21-22), thus stating her belief in Jesus' power as a miracle worker and as someone having great influence with God. When Jesus asserts that "your brother will rise" (11:23), Martha takes his statement as the conventional Jewish belief in resurrection of the dead as part of the scenario of events connected with the full coming of God's kingdom—a belief shared by the Pharisees and other Jewish groups: "I know he will rise, in the resurrection on the last day" (11:24). In proclaiming himself to be "the resurrection and the life" (11:25), Jesus makes himself the point of reference for the resurrection and suggests that through faith in him, eternal life (the resurrection) has already begun (11:26). Though Martha asserts that she believes this, her response in 11:27 in which she uses titles appropriate to what the Gospel has taught so far ("you are the Messiah, the Son of God, the one who is coming into the world") shows that she does not yet comprehend what it means to confess Jesus as "the resurrection and the life."

The fourth segment (11:28-37) begins as the third segment did. Mary approaches Jesus and states that, if Jesus had been there, Lazarus would not have died (11:32; see 11:21). The major difference is that here the "Jews" who had been comforting Mary accompany her and serve as witnesses both to Jesus' reaction and to his raising of Lazarus from the dead (11:31). The parallelism breaks off at 11:33-36 to focus on Jesus' emotional attachment to Lazarus—an unusual element in John's Gospel. Jesus' display of emotion leads the "Jews" who function a kind of chorus here to affirm that Jesus had given sight to the man born blind (see 9:1-12) and that he could have prevented Lazarus from dying. Though it does not advance the plot significantly, this segment provides an emotional engagement on Jesus' part and adds to the suspense that will be resolved in the final segment

The last segment (11:38-44) describes the removal of the stone from the mouth of the tomb (11:38-39), states the purpose of the raising of Lazarus (11:40), recounts Jesus' prayer (11:41-42), and tells about the revival of Lazarus (11:43-44). The resurrection of Lazarus to life is a sign of Jesus' own resurrection and his power to give eternal life to others. However, it is only a sign, since it is assumed that Lazarus will again suffer physical death. The description of the tomb and its stone (11:38-39) and of the burial garments (11:44) points forward to the empty tomb story in John 20:1-10. The emphasis on "the glory of God" (11:40) prepares for the presentation of the passion as the hour of Jesus' exaltation. Jesus is so close to the Father that he really does not need to pray; he does it only as a pedagogical device for the crowd (11:41-42).

The Plot Against Jesus (11:45-57)

The foolish boast made by Thomas in 11:16 ("Let us go to die with him") has already linked the Lazarus episode near Jerusalem and the plot against Jesus by the Jewish officials. The remainder of chapter 11 explains how that plot took shape and developed.

The initial reaction among the "Jews" was divided (see 7:12-13; 7:43; 10:19). Whereas some begin to believe in Jesus (11:45), others report to the Pharisees what Jesus had done (11:46). With this report, John leaves behind the favorable description of the "Jews" in 11:1-44 and presents the Pharisees as the chief plotters against Jesus.

In response to the Pharisees' concerns, the Sanhedrin is convened. In the other Gospels, this meeting takes place after Jesus' arrest and shortly before his hearing before Pilate (Mark 14:53-65; Matt 26:57-68; Luke 22:66-71). John probably overstates the historical influence of the Pharisees with the Sanhedrin, which in Jesus' time was dominated by chief priests, elders, and scribes. The fear expressed by the chief priests and Pharisees in 11:48 is that "the Romans will come and take away both our land and our nation"—precisely what did occur in A.D. 70. The practical advice given by Caiaphas ("that one man should die instead of the people, so that the whole nation may not perish") turns into a Christian prophecy of Jesus' death and its significance (11:49-52). Caiaphas was high priest from A.D. 18 to 36. The description of him as "high priest for that year" (11:51) need not imply an annual change of high priests (which was not the case). Rather, Caiaphas happened to be high priest in "that year" when Jesus died. The narrator observes that Jesus died not only for the nation of Israel, but also "to gather into one the dispersed children of God" (11:52)— perhaps a reference to Jews in the Diaspora (outside the land of Israel) or to Gentiles seeking to be part of God's people (see 10:16). So the desire to avoid trouble from the Romans provides the occasion for the plot to kill Jesus (11:53).

The development of the plot leads to a second withdrawal on Jesus' part (see 10:40)—this time to a town called Ephraim (11:54), which is some twelve miles northeast of Jerusalem. As the third Passover of Jesus' public ministry (see 2:13; 6:4) approaches, there is speculation among the general populace whether Jesus will make the pilgrimage (11:56) and an order by the chief priests and Pharisees that Jesus should be turned in and arrested (11:57). The division of opinions with which the passage began turns into a firm plot against Jesus on the officials' part. The "hour" of Jesus is approaching.

Anointing at Bethany and Entry into Jerusalem (12:1-19)

The events surrounding Jesus' final Passover begin with the

anointing of Jesus at Bethany (12:3-8) and his entry into Jerusalem (12:12-16). Both episodes are recounted in the other Gospels, though there the entry precedes the anointing. In John's Gospel, these episodes are framed by reports that mention Lazarus (12:1-2, 9-11, 17-19), thus continuing the connection between Jesus' restoring Lazarus to life and his death.

The Jewish celebration of Passover combined the spring agricultural festival (Unleavened Bread) and the commemoration of Israel's liberation from slavery in Egypt. When the Jerusalem temple stood, Passover was a pilgrimage feast that featured solemn assemblies at the temple. After the temple was destroyed in A.D. 70, the focus shifted to celebrating the Passover meal in private homes. Leviticus 23:5-8 describes the timing and services of Passover in biblical times:

> The Passover of the Lord falls on the fourteenth day of the first month, at the evening twilight. The fifteenth day of this month is the Lord's feast of Unleavened Bread. For seven days you shall eat unleavened bread. On the first of these days you shall hold a sacred assembly and do no sort of work. On each of the seven days you shall offer an oblation to the Lord. Then on the seventh day you shall again hold a sacred assembly and do no sort of work.

The anointing is located at Bethany (near Jerusalem), six days before Passover (12:1). It takes place at a dinner in which Martha serves (see Luke 10:40) and Lazarus appears at table with Jesus (12:2). The public appearance of Lazarus at this dinner confirms the fact that Jesus restored him to life.

The anointing itself (12:3-8) shares some features with the accounts in Mark 14:3-9 and Matt 26:6-13: the description of the ointment ("costly perfumed oil made from genuine aromatic nard"), the value at three-hundred denarii, and Jesus' saying about always having the poor among us. In Luke 7:36-50, a sinful woman anoints Jesus at the house of Simon the leper, and in response Jesus pronounces her sins forgiven. In John 12:3-8, Mary of Bethany does the anointing. Though in Christian tradition, Mary of Bethany has been linked with both the sinful woman of Luke 7:36-50 and Mary Magdalene of John 20:11-18, there is no reason to equate these three figures.

The focus of the episode is the anointing. It was odd to anoint someone's feet (the head was more usually anointed) and to use so much that the oil had to be wiped off (12:3). That Mary's action was intended to be symbolic is indicated by the interpretation given to it by Jesus: "Let her keep this for the day of my burial" (12:7). At the end of chapter 11, the Sanhedrin had decided that Jesus must die (11:53, 57); now Mary's action prepares Jesus' body for burial—even down to his feet. Mary applied the precious ointment so lavishly that she had to wipe away the excess with her hair. Her generosity and enthusiasm contrast with the calculating attitude displayed by Judas, who argues that the oil could have been sold for three-hundred days' pay (12:5; see Matt 20:2). While championing the tradition of giving alms to the poor, Judas is also fleeing from the idea of Jesus as a suffering Messiah who will soon meet death. Only John among the Evangelists charges that Judas was stealing from the common purse of Jesus and his disciples (12:6).

Between the anointing at Bethany and the entry into Jerusalem, there is another notice about Lazarus (12:9-11), which underscores the connection between the Lazarus episode and Jesus' death. Lazarus has become such an attraction that many of the "Jews" come to believe in Jesus (12:9, 11). Therefore, the chief priests plot to kill Lazarus, too (12:10).

In John's chronology, Jesus' entry into Jerusalem (12:12-16) follows the anointing, whereas in the other Gospels it precedes the anointing. The basic story is the same in all four Gospels. Jesus is greeted in Jerusalem by a crowd that shouts out the pilgrims' greeting from Ps 118:25-26: "Blessed is he who comes in the name of the Lord" (12:13). For his entrance, Jesus rides on a young donkey (12:14-15), thus acting out what is said in Zech 9:9 (see Matt 21:5). The distinctive features of the Johannine account include the following: The crowd bears palm branches (12:13) used to welcome conquerors (see 1 Macc 13:51; 2 Macc 10:7); the crowd goes out to meet Jesus (12:13); Jesus is hailed as "the king of Israel" (12:13); and the disciples fail to understand (12:16). These Johannine emphases prepare for the portrayal of Jesus as a king throughout the passion, despite all appearances. Only after the "hour" of Jesus' glorification—his passion, death, resurrection, and ascension—would the disciples grasp the full significance of his entry into Jerusalem.

The final notice about Lazarus (12:17-19) concerns the crowd that witnessed his restoration to life. John relates the enthusiastic reception that Jesus received on entering Jerusalem to the reports about that "sign" (12:18). In frustration the Pharisees observe: "Look, the whole world has gone after him" (12:19). With irony they actually "prophesy" (see 11:51) the universal significance of Jesus and the universal mission of the church. In the other Gospels, the cleansing of the temple follows Jesus' entry into Jerusalem. But John had already told that story in 2:13-22.

With these episodes before Passover, John has set the stage for the passion of Jesus. The anointing of Jesus prepares for his death and burial. The entry into Jerusalem reveals who Jesus really is: the king of Israel. The Lazarus notices that frame the central episodes carry on the irony that giving life back leads to Jesus' death. They also highlight the division within Israel: Some believe in Jesus, but the Pharisees continue to plot his death because "the whole world has gone after him."

The End of Jesus' Public Ministry (12:20-50)

The remainder of chapter 12 brings to conclusion the public ministry of Jesus. Jesus first engages in dialogue with Andrew and Philip as representatives of certain "Greeks" and with the "crowd" (12:20-36). Then the Evangelist gives some explanations why the "Jews" refuse to believe in Jesus (12:37-43). The final section summarizes what the first twelve chapters have taught about Jesus' person and mission (12:44-50).

The first part of the dialogue (12:20-33) is set in motion by the request of "some Greeks" who wish to see Jesus and use Philip and Andrew as intermediaries (12:20-22). The exact identity of these "Greeks" is not clear. Most likely they are not Greeks in the ethnic sense. Rather, they may have been Greek-speaking Jews from the Diaspora, or prospective converts to Judaism, or "God-fearers" (Gentiles) interested in Judaism. Their request coincides with the arrival of the "hour" in which Jesus as Son of Man will be glorified (12:23). The "Greeks" get left behind as Jesus proceeds to relate the hour of his glorification to his suffering and death by means of sayings: the grain of wheat that dies and thus produces fruit (12:24), losing one's life to save it (12:25), and serving Jesus in discipleship (12:26). Though these sayings seem to have been traditional (see 1 Cor 15:36-37; Mark 8:34-35), there are some distinctive Johannine accents: the contrast between "this world" and "eternal life" (12:25), and the idea that the Father will honor those who serve Jesus (12:26). In a manner that evokes the Gethsemane scene (Mark 14:32-42), Jesus contemplates asking the Father to save him from this hour (12:27). But then he reaffirms his commitment to accept his hour and asks God to "glorify your name." In response, a heavenly voice says: "I have glorified it and will glorify it again" (12:28). Just as God's name had been glorified in the signs done by Jesus, so in the "hour" of Jesus (his passion, death, resurrection, and exaltation) God's name will be glorified again. Even though the heavenly voice was intended for the benefit of the crowd, they fail to understand it (12:29-30). Their misunderstanding leads to further explanation on Jesus' part (12:31-33). His "hour" means the driving out of the "ruler of this world" (Satan), thus recalling the dualistic schema laid out in John 3:16-21. His "lifting up" in crucifixion will mean the possibility of exaltation and glorification for all. There is very likely a play on the terms used for describing crucifixion as a lifting up and Jesus' resurrection-exaltation.

In the final part of the dialogue (12:34-36), the crowd again shows its failure to understand Jesus by objecting that there must be a contradiction between the lifting up of the Son of Man and the tradition that the Messiah remains forever (12:34). The assumption of the dialogue is that Jesus had been speaking of himself as the Son of Man (see 12:23, and perhaps in 12:32). The biblical passages that come closest to affirming that the Messiah will remain forever are Psalms 61:8 ("let him [the king] sit enthroned before God forever") and 89:3 ("His [David's] posterity shall continue forever"). Jesus cuts the debate short (12:35-36) by appealing to the light-darkness imagery (see 9:4; 11:9-10) and urging the crowd to believe in the Light (see 1:5, 9) and so become children of the light (see 3:19). On saying this, Jesus left and hid from them, thus ending his public ministry.

A major question facing the Evangelist (and other early Christians) was, Why have not all Jews accepted Jesus? Even on the part of those who witnessed Jesus' signs, the response was not uniformly one of belief. Why? John's first explanation (12:37-41) draws on two quotations from the book of Isaiah. According to Isa 53:1, not everyone believed the revelation of God's Suffering Servant. Likewise, not everyone believed the revelation of God's Son (12:38). According to Isa 6:9-10, God willed that not all would believe the prophet's message. This fact, revealed to Isaiah in his vision of God's glory (Isa 6:1), really referred by way of prophecy to the response that Jesus got from the "Jews." To the "biblical" explanation John adds a more immediate, political rationale: The Pharisees put pressure on those who believed in Jesus by threatening to expel them from the synagogue (12:42-43).

The final section (12:44-50) recapitulates what we have learned about Jesus thus far. Since Jesus had gone into hiding (12:36), no audience is mentioned. Jesus has been sent by his heavenly Father. Whoever believes in him and sees him, believes in and sees the Father (12:44-45). He is the Light come into the world (12:46) to save the world (12:47). Those who reject his word already have their judge (God) and will be judged on the last day—a combination of anticipated and final eschatology (12:48). At the end (12:49-50) Jesus returns to his role as the emissary of the Father. The "commandment" given him by the Father leads to eternal life. Thus, the Gospel places in perspective what Jesus had done publicly by teaching and performing signs: As the revealer of God, Jesus was sent to make manifest who God is and what God wills.

III

Jesus' Farewells To His Disciples (13:1-17:27)

The Footwashing (13:1-20)

With the end of his public ministry, Jesus turns to the instruction of his disciples at the Last Supper. The farewell discourses in chapters 13-17 provide interpretations of Jesus' death and indicate how his disciples are to carry on when he is no longer physically among them.

Chapter 13 sets the scene for the farewell discourses. Its double focus is (1) the noble Jesus who lays down his life as an example for his disciples and (2) the obtuse and treacherous disciples (Judas and Peter). There are loose parallels to these incidents in the other Gospels. Only with chapter 18 will the narrative of the other Gospels be rejoined. The intervening speeches (chapters 14-17) are unique to John.

The Last Supper, according to John 13:1, took place some twenty-four hours before the eight-day Passover festival began. Jesus died on the next afternoon, when the Passover lambs were being sacrificed in the temple, just before the start of the actual Passover celebration at dusk. The other Evangelists suggest that the Last Supper was the Passover meal, whereas John presents it as a meal with Passover themes and characteristics (like having a Christmas party on December 23 or 24). John's information about the dating of Jesus' Last Supper and death is probably accurate.

The chronological indicator in John 13:1 ("before the feast

of Passover") is accompanied by a rich theological interpretation of Jesus' death. It is his "hour" at last. His death is a return to the Father. It is the ultimate proof of his love for his disciples ("he loved them to the end"). These themes run through chapters 13-17, and their appearance here serves as a kind of program for what follows.

The footwashing symbolizes Jesus' service on his disciples' behalf (13:2-5). By mentioning Judas' betrayal at the outset (13:2), the Evangelist places Jesus' action in connection with his death. By attributing Judas' treachery to the devil ("the devil had already induced Judas"), he sets Jesus' death in the cosmic, dualistic framework that he had developed throughout the Gospel. The following verse (13:3) outlines the whole of John's understanding of Jesus: "fully aware that the Father had put everything into his power and that he had come from God and was returning to God." After this introduction, the act of footwashing is described very briefly (13:4-5). Jesus does what a slave might be expected to do, thus "taking the form of a slave" (Phil 2:7). Since John omits Jesus' institution of the Lord's Supper (see Mark 14:22-25), the footwashing serves as the symbolic action used to cast light on the meaning of his death on the cross.

The first explanation of the footwashing comes in the dialogue with Peter (13:6-11). Peter's initial protest in 13:6 ("Master, are you going to wash my feet?") is met with an assurance from Jesus that afterward (after Jesus' passion, death, resurrection, and exaltation), he would understand (13:7). Peter's more vehement resistance ("You will never wash my feet") in 13:8 receives a more explicit response from Jesus: "Unless I wash you, you will have no inheritance with me." With the humbling act of washing the feet of others, Jesus had indicated that he would undergo the humiliation of crucifixion. Now he insists that his death has significance for the disciples and that they must accept his humble service. Thus, Peter is challenged to accept the gift of salvation that comes in the form of Jesus' humble service. When Peter does get the point (13:9), he demands even more than he has received ("not only my feet, but my hands and head as well"). Jesus in turn corrects Peter by insisting that what he had done was sufficient that the disciples be clean. The parenthetical phrase ("except to have his feet washed") is absent from many manuscripts; it may have been inserted to reflect the practice of footwashing as a kind of "sacramental" gesture in some communities. The first explanation ends with a reference to Judas as the betrayer ("not all of you are clean") and asserts that Jesus knew it beforehand. So the first explanation challenges Jesus' disciples to accept his humble death as a saving action and to believe that it has saving significance for their lives.

The second explanation (13:12-20) presents the footwashing as an example that the disciples can follow as they deal with fellow disciples. Now Jesus speaks directly to his disciples. If he as their master and teacher has performed this humble act (footwashing, death on the cross) on their behalf, how much more should they be willing to serve one another! He has given them a "model to follow" (13:15)

This positive instruction on discipleship as service of others is balanced off by another warning about Judas' betrayal (13:18-19), which is connected with Psalm 41:10 ("The one who ate my food has raised his heel against me") and with the revelation of Jesus' identity as "I AM." Jesus concludes (13:20) by establishing a chain of "sending" and "receiving": Whoever receives his disciples receives him and the one who sent him (see Matt 10:40; Mark 9:37; Luke 9:48; 10:16). The second explanation challenges the disciples to imitate Jesus' action of loving service.

Prophecies of Betrayal and the New Commandment (13:21-38)

After Jesus' direct address in 13:12-20, the text reverts to dialogue between Jesus and his disciples. The remainder of chapter 13 consists of the prophecy of Judas' betrayal of Jesus (13:21-30), Jesus' teaching about his glorification and the new commandment of love (13:31-35), and the prophecy of Peter's denial (13:36-38). The effect of this ABA1 structure is to contrast the nobility of Jesus and the treachery of his disciples.

The announcement of Judas' betrayal of Jesus (13:21-30) is

given more attention and specificity than in the other Gospels (Mark 14:18-21; Matt 26:21-25; Luke 22:21-23). The betrayer is clearly identified as Judas, at least to the "beloved disciple" and to the reader. As in the other Gospels, Jesus states that one of the disciples will betray him—an announcement that sends them into confusion and puzzlement (13:21-22). The unique feature of John's account is the dialogue between Jesus and an unnamed disciple, known only as "the one whom Jesus loved" (13:23). The "beloved disciple" appears again at the cross (19:26-27), at the empty tomb (20:2), and in the Galilean appearances of the risen Lord (21:7, 20). He has been identified as John the son of Zebedee, Lazarus, the Evangelist, and/or the "ideal disciple." But he remains a mysterious figure. As the group reclined on couches, the beloved disciple was in a place of honor, beside Jesus (see 1:18). Only he seems to learn the identity of Jesus' betrayer. By giving a choice morsel to Judas, Jesus answers the beloved disciple's question. Nevertheless, the Evangelist places Judas' betrayal in a larger framework: "After he took the morsel, Satan entered him" (13:27). The disciples miss the point of Jesus' action and his exchange with Judas (13:28-29). The final verse ("So he took the morsel and left at once. And it was night," 13:30) emphasizes that Jesus knew beforehand about his betrayal, that Judas rejected the offer of discipleship and willingly betrayed Jesus, and that he was the instrument of Satan and the "night."

After the prophecy of betrayal by Judas, Jesus interprets the meaning of his death (13:31-33) and instructs the disciples on how his movement might be carried on (13:34-35). Jesus' death on the cross will—despite all appearances—be a glorification. As Son of Man he will be glorified, and thus God will glorify him (13:31). In response God will glorify the Son of Man "at once"—in the resurrection. By his obedience and self-sacrificing love, Jesus glorifies God. By raising Jesus from the dead, God reveals his glory in Jesus more dramatically than in any of the signs. Now Jesus' mysterious sayings to the "Jews" about going away (7:33; 8:21) become clear: They refer to his exaltation, a process that includes suffering, death, resurrection, and ascension to glory. The period of Jesus' personal presence among the disciples is coming to a close (13:33).

How the disciples are to carry on without the earthly Jesus is addressed by the "new commandment": "Love one another" (13:34). It is hard to grasp the sense in which this commandment is "new," since the command to love one's neighbor appears in Lev 19:18 and in several New Testament texts (Mark 12:31; Matt 22:39; Luke 10:27; 1 Thess 4:9; Gal 5:14; Rom 13:9). At any rate, the loving service of others will keep alive the spirit of Jesus. What is imagined is a "chain" of loving service: "As I have loved you, so you also should love one another" (13:34). This is the lesson of the footwashing (13:2-20). This is to be the sign of the community of Jesus (13:35). The focus of this loving service seems to be other members of the community. The love manifested in the inner circle will be recognized by outsiders as the distinguishing feature of the followers of Jesus.

Jesus' prophecy of Peter's denial (13:36-38) looks backward to his prophecy about Judas (13:21-30) and forward to the narrative of Peter's denial (18:15-18, 25-27). In John's account (see Mark 14:26-31; Matt 26:30-35; Luke 22:31-34), Peter picks up on Jesus' still mysterious (to him) saying about his departure. Peter wants to know where Jesus is going (13:36). Jesus replies that Peter cannot follow him now, though he will do so later on—probably an anticipation of what is suggested about Peter's own death in 21:18-19. When Peter protests that he is willing to die for Jesus right now (13:37), Jesus predicts that Peter will deny him three times before dawn that night (13:38). Peter has still not learned the lesson of the footwashing (13:6-11)—that he must accept the gift of salvation on Jesus' terms and in God's own time.

The contrast between the noble Jesus and the treacherous disciples prepares for the two major themes in the farewell discourses of chapters 14 through 17. These speeches concern the identity of Jesus and the way of discipleship. More particularly, they explore how the movement begun by Jesus can continue when he is no longer physically present among his disciples.

Assurances and Promises (14:1-31)

With chapter 14 the Fourth Gospel begins a series of farewell

discourses that extend through chapter 17. Only with the betrayal and arrest of Jesus in 18:1-11 is the sequence of events
found in the other Gospels rejoined. These farewell discourses
serve the same basic functions as the eschatological discourses
(Mark 13, Matthew 24-25, Luke 21) do in the other Gospels:
They tell about the future, when the earthly Jesus is no longer
among his disciples. But the Johannine farewell discourses are
more concerned with the immediate and continuing future
than they are with the end of human history and the coming of
God's kingdom.

In literary form, John 14 carries on the pattern set in chapter
13. Jesus' statements are misunderstood by his disciples whose
questions or observations (14:5, 8, 22) provide the occasion for
Jesus to explain himself more fully. These statements are
mainly assurances to the disciples about the importance of
faith and love, as well as promises that the disciples will receive
divine help in the absence of the earthly Jesus. No neat outline
manages to take in the entire content of the passage. But the
text clearly provides assurances (14:1-11, 15-26) and promises
(14:12-14, 27-31).

The first set of assurances (14:1-11) begins with a word of
encouragement ("Do not let your hearts be troubled"), which
recurs toward the end of this speech (14:27). Jesus stresses the
importance of faith in God and faith in him (14:1), which, in
light of his teaching thus far in the Gospel, are virtually the
same since Jesus is the one who reveals God. In 14:2-3 Jesus
picks up his talk about going away from the end of chapter 13.
The goal of Jesus' going away in death is to prepare a place for
his own in glory with God. His being fully united with God in
glory makes it possible for others to be united with God. In an
unusual Johannine reference to the parousia or second coming,
Jesus promises: "I will come back again and take you to
myself" (14:3).

When Jesus announces that the disciples know the way
(14:4), Thomas protests that, since they do not know where
Jesus is going, they also do not know the way (14:5). Jesus
answers by proclaiming himself "the way and the truth and the
life" (14:6). As the revealer of God, Jesus shows the way of
access to God. In his person and works, the truth of God is

incarnate. He is the source of the eternal life that begins in the present. Thus, the disciples are assured that through Jesus, they are on the one way that leads to the Father: "No one comes to the Father except through me" (14:6). In the late first-century conflict with other Jews, such a statement would have emphasized the correctness of the Christian way and the shortcomings of the other ways (apocalypticism, Torah observance) being proposed.

Next Jesus assures the disciples that they will know the Father since they have known him (14:7). During Jesus' public ministry, the disciples found much hard to understand. As his "hour" approaches, they will be given the key to understanding Jesus more perfectly. In light of Jesus' passion, death, resurrection, and exaltation, they will know about Jesus and God. Philip's naive request ("show us the Father," 14:8) serves as the occasion for Jesus to insist that those who have seen him have seen the Father (14:9). The Father is in Jesus and works through him (14:10) to such an extent that Jesus can proclaim: "I am in the Father and the Father is in me" (14:10, 11).

Thus far, Jesus has assured the disciples of a place with God, the way to God, and perfect knowledge of God. All these assurances rest upon the person of Jesus. He goes to prepare a place for his own. He provides the way to God, since he is the way. To know him (especially in his "hour") is to know God, since there is a mutual indwelling.

Jesus promises that his disciples will do great works (14:12) and that their prayers in his name will be answered (14:13-14). The "works" are signs that reveal God. Those who believe in Jesus carry on the tradition begun by him. The idea that they will do even "greater" works alludes back to Jesus' promise to Nathanael in 1:50 ("You will see greater things than this") and his claim before the "Jews" in 5:20 ("he will show him greater works than these"). The promise looks forward to the time after Easter as the age of great signs. All this is possible because "I am going to the Father."

Jesus also promises that the prayers of his disciples will be answered. The almost automatic effectiveness of the prayer of petition is emphasized in Matt 7:7-11 and Luke 11:9-13. The distinctively Johannine treatment of this theme in 14:13-14 focuses attention on the person of Jesus. The prayer is "in my name." The one who responds to the petition is Jesus ("I will do it," 14:13, 14). The goal of the prayer and Jesus' response to it is "so that the Father may be glorified in the Son." Whereas the other biblical writers focus their theology of prayer on the Father, John looks to Jesus (in whom the Father dwells) as the catalyst for effective prayer.

The second set of assurances (14:15-26) seems to begin and end with references to the Paraclete, who is identified as the Holy Spirit (14:17, 26). In fact, the structure is more intricate than is suggested by that perception. The main unit (14:15-21) follows a chiastic outline (ABB1A1), and the remaining parts (14:22-24; 14:25-26) offer comments on the two main topics (AB). The two main topics are (A) keeping the commandments as an expression of loving Jesus, and (B) living in the future. Both topics are raised as ways of keeping alive the movement begun by the earthly Jesus.

In the main unit, Jesus begins by (A) announcing that those who love him will keep his commandments (14:15). Although the Johannine Jesus does not define precisely what these commandments are, one can presume that they include belief in him and love toward others—the heart of the teachings of the Johannine Jesus. By keeping Jesus' commandments of faith and love, his disciples will keep his movement alive.

The first promise of the Paraclete (B) in 14:16-17 explains how the disciples are to carry on in the future without the earthly Jesus: God will provide "another Advocate" in his place. The Greek term *parakletos* ("one called to the side of") has a legal sense as "defense attorney" or "spokesman." But the legal background does not exhaust the meaning. According to 1 John 2:1, Jesus is our Paraclete or Advocate with the Father. Thus, the Spirit of Truth is "another Advocate" who serves as a "stand-in" for the earthly Jesus and remains among his disciples. The "world" (those forces opposed to Jesus and his own) cannot accept the Spirit because it neither sees nor knows it.

To what does 14:18-20 (B1) refer—Jesus' resurrection, or his second coming? While for many interpreters, it refers to the appearances of the risen Lord, to me it seems more reasonable to connect it with the "day of the Lord" and the parousia. This interpretation is indicated by certain phrases in the text ("I will come to you" .... "on that day") and by a similar juxtaposition of realized and final eschatologies in 5:20-27. If so, 14:18-20 functions as the mirror (B1) of the first Paraclete promise (14:16-17). The Spirit of Truth guides the community of Jesus' disciples in the present. The hope of Jesus' return on the last day gives them the trust and confidence to face the present, knowing that the future is secure.

The final part of the main unit (14:21) repeats Jesus' admonition that those who love him will keep his commandments. But it grounds the admonition in a "chain" of love and revelation: "And whoever loves me will be loved by my Father, and I will love him and reveal myself to him."

The additional comment on the first topic (14:22-24)—love for Jesus shown in keeping his commandments—is generated by the question of Judas, presumably the son of James (see Luke 6:16; Acts 1:13). He asks why the revelation of Jesus is not more public, why it is only to his own and not to the world (14:22). Jesus' somewhat indirect reply (14:23-24) insists that the Father and the Son are present where love for Jesus and fidelity to his teaching are present.

The additional comment on the Paraclete (14:25-26) specifies the role of the Holy Spirit as the "stand-in" for Jesus: The Paraclete will teach the community and remind it of Jesus' own teaching. On the one hand, the Spirit equips the disciples to face new situations without the earthly Jesus. On the other hand, the Spirit's guidance is in continuity with the teaching of the earthly Jesus; it is what Jesus would have taught in the circumstances.

Before departing, Jesus promises his peace (14:27)—the wholeness, the eternal life already begun through him and carried on by the Paraclete. By way of conclusion, Jesus provides another interpretation of his death. It is an occasion for joy, since Jesus returns to his Father, who is described as "greater than I" (14:28) because he sent Jesus to reveal him and Jesus bears witness to him. Jesus' death will also be the proof to the world of Jesus' love for the Father and his perfect obedience to him (14:31).

The discourse in chapter 14 breaks off with Jesus' command "Get up, let us go" (14:31). Since the "ruler of the world" (Satan) is coming, Jesus' attitude is both defiant ("he has no power over me") and eager to move into his "hour." If one flips over to John 18:1, there would be perfect literary continuity. But our present version of John's Gospel provides three more chapters of "farewell" discourses in which the departing Jesus instructs his followers on how to carry on his movement.

Love and Hate (15:1-16:4)

In the second farewell discourse, Jesus emphasizes the love that should prevail within the community of his disciples (15:1-17) and warns against the hate that will be displayed toward it from outside (15:18-16:4). In both parts, ideas raised in chapter 14 are expanded and developed.

Jesus' monologue about love within the community (15:1-17) begins with the allegory of the vine (15:1-6) and ends with an intricately structured commentary on abiding in Jesus (15:7-17).

When Jesus proclaimed himself as the "vine," he appealed not only to the experience of Jews in first-century Palestine but also to the biblical heritage. Psalm 80:9-17 identifies Israel as the vine of God and traces its history from the exodus to the exile:

> A vine from Egypt you transplanted;
>   you drove away the nations and
>   planted it.
> You cleared the ground for it,
>   and it took root and filled the land.
> The mountains were hidden in its
>   shadow;
>   by its branches, the cedars of God.
> It put forth its foliage to the Sea,
>   its shoots as far as the River.

Why have you broken down its walls,
so that every passer-by plucks its
fruit,
The boar from the forest lays it
waste,
and the beasts of the field feed
upon it?
Once again, O Lord of hosts,
look down from heaven, and see;
Take care of this vine,
and protect what your right hand
has planted
[the son of man whom you yourself
made strong].

Let those who would burn it with fire
or cut it down
perish before you at your rebuke.

The allegory of the vine has its background in Old Testament passages that depict Israel as God's vine (Ps 80:9-17; Jer 2:21; Ezek 15:2; 17:5-10; 19:10; Hos 10:1) and identify the vine as Wisdom (Sir 24:17) or the Son of Man (Ps 80:16). The figure of speech is an allegory because each entity is equated with someone: the vine is Jesus, the farmer/vine grower is God, and the branches are those who follow Jesus. Jesus is the vine (15:1) in the sense that his vital power courses through the whole plant and serves as its source of life. The Father is the "vine grower" or "farmer" (*geōrgos*) who tends to the vine at every stage of its existence. The disciples are the branches and so depend upon both the vine and the vine grower for their life and care.

One of the vine grower's chief activities is cutting away the dead branches (15:2a) and pruning the live branches so that these produce even more abundant fruit (15:2b). In Greek there is a pun on the words for "take away" (*airein*) and "prune" (*katharein*). The criterion by which the branches live or die is their bearing fruit, presumably by keeping Jesus' commandments to believe and to love. The disciples to whom Jesus speaks are already "pruned" (*katharoi*) through his word (15:3); that is, they are cleansed from all that prevents them from bearing fruit.

In 15:4-6 the vine allegory is linked with the familiar Johannine theme of "abiding" or "remaining" in Jesus. Just as the branch cannot bear fruit unless it remains on the vine, so Jesus' disciples cannot bear fruit unless they abide in him. Those that fail to abide in Jesus can expect to be cut off, to wither up, and to be burned up as fuel for the fire. The vine allegory in John 15:1-6 teaches that believers/disciples are related to Jesus in a vital way, and that their discipleship entails abiding in that relationship and demands faithfulness.

It is possible to take 15:7-17 as an intricately structured commentary on abiding in Jesus, with the theme of joy (15:11) at the center: A—all my words (15:7a); B—ask for whatever you want (15:7b); C—bearing fruit (15:8a); D—becoming disciples (15:8b); E—the "chain" of love (15:9); F—keeping my commandments and love (15:10); G—joy (15:11); F1—my commandment is love (15:12); E1—the greatest love (15:13); D1—becoming friends (15:14-15); C1—bearing fruit (15:16a); B1—ask for whatever you want (15:16b); A1—the love commandment (15:17).

This commentary insists repeatedly on the love commandment: "love one another as I have loved you . . . . love one another" (15:12, 17). It roots love for one another in the perfect example of self-sacrificing love soon to be displayed by Jesus: "No one has greater love than this, to lay down one's life for one's friends" (15:13). These emphases may have some connection to the crisis within the Johannine community that is the subject of 1 John. In that situation, there seems to be an effort to disregard the sufferings of Jesus and a failure in mutual love within the community.

The commentary also provides a powerful understanding of discipleship. The disciples of Jesus (15:8b) are his "friends" (15:14). They have been chosen by him (15:16), contrary to the usual procedure by which disciples chose their master (see John 1:35-51). They exist in a "chain of love": "As the Father loves me, so I also love you. Remain in my love" (15:9). Their task is to "bear fruit" (15:16), confident that what they ask in prayer will be granted (15:7b, 16b). The goal of Jesus in his teaching is perfect joy: "so that my joy might be in you and your joy might be complete" (15:11).

The stress on love within the community is balanced by a reflection on hatred from outside the community in 15:18-16:4. The chief enemy outside the community is the "world." In John's Gospel the term "world" (*kosmos*) can be used in a neutral or even positive sense (see 3:16). But it can also carry a negative sense as it does here to describe the hostile forces arrayed against Jesus and his disciples. In this context, there is a sharp break between the "world" and the community of Jesus' disciples.

The first part (15:18-20) roots the world's hatred for the disciples in its hatred for Jesus. By choosing his disciples, Jesus has taken them out of the world and so made them subject to the world's hatred of him: "If the world hates you, realize that it hated me first" (15:18). On the other hand, since the disciples belong to Jesus, they must experience what he experienced before them—even persecution (15:20). The section ends on a curious note: "If they kept my word, they will also keep yours." This line is best treated as irony. Since the world has not kept Jesus' word at all, the disciples can expect a similar non-acceptance for their word.

The reasons for the world's hatred of Jesus and his disciples are considered in 15:21-25: The world does not know the one who sent Jesus (15:21); by hating Jesus it hates the Father (15:23, 24); its hatred fulfills Psalm 35:19 (or 69:5): "They hated me without cause." Just as the Father, Jesus, and his disciples share in a "chain" of love (see 15:9), so they also share in a "chain" of hatred from the world. The coming of Jesus has brought about a "crisis" for the world in the root sense of the term *krisis* ("judgment, decision"). In light of Jesus' person and activity, the world has no excuse for its sin (15:22). Despite Jesus' unprecedented "signs," the world has fallen more deeply into sin, because it hates Jesus and his Father (15:24).

Yet the community of Jesus' disciples is not alone in its struggle against the world. Now it has Jesus himself. When he leaves, the Advocate or Paraclete will take his place (15:26).

The Advocate (the "Spirit of truth") proceeds from the Father and is sent by the Son. Here the Advocate's role is to bear witness to Jesus and to empower the disciples who had been with Jesus "from the beginning" (see 1 John 1:1) to give witness themselves. In the context of trial and judgment (*krisis*), the Advocate serves as the defense attorney and facilitates the testimony of the disciples (see Matt 10:18-20).

Concrete examples of the world's hatred are given in 16:1-4. The examples are framed by explanations why Jesus is telling these things to his followers: "that you may not fall away" (16:1); "that when their hour comes you may remember that I told you" (16:4). The two examples of the world's hatred are expulsion from the synagogues and persecution ending in death. The first punishment seems to have been carried out in the historical experience of the Johannine community (see John 9:22; 12:42). Whether the Johannine community had suffered death for the name of Jesus is less certain. Persecution against the early Christian community was a reality, and Stephen in Acts 7:54-60 appears to be a martyr. Yet there is no record of a universal, systematic persecution of the early church. Rather, what active persecution there was tended to be local and sporadic. But at least the threat of persecution may have been present to the Johannine community. Jesus' own fate would have led it to take seriously even the threat of death for the Christian faith.

Jesus' Departure and Return (16:5-33)

The third farewell discourse (16:5-33) reflects on various aspects of Jesus' departure and return: why it is good for him to go away (16:5-15), sorrow at his departure and joy at his return (16:16-24), and Jesus' use of figurative and plain speech (16:25-33).

Jesus' warnings about exclusion from the synagogue and persecution unto death in 15:18-16:4 have the effect of filling the disciples with sorrow over their own situation (16:6) and distracting them from the more important question about Jesus' departure: "Not one of you asks me 'Where are you going?'" (16:5). Jesus comes back to his own departure by explaining why it is advantageous for his disciples that he leave them (16:7). Since the Advocate or Paraclete is the "stand-in" for the earthly Jesus in the community and cannot be present in the same place at the same time, therefore Jesus must depart so that the Paraclete might come. The departure of the earthly Jesus and the arrival of the Paraclete will enhance rather than diminish Jesus' presence among his own.

Whereas in the other Paraclete texts (14:15-17; 14:26; 15:26; 16:13-14) the community is the arena of activity, here the "world" taken in a negative sense is the object of the Paraclete's work. That work is prosecutorial. The Paraclete will convict the world (16:8) regarding "sin" by showing that its refusal to believe in Jesus is the root of sin (16:9), regarding "righteousness" by showing that the world's unjust condemnation of Jesus will not thwart the victory of Jesus as he returns to the Father (16:10), and regarding judgment or condemnation by showing that Jesus' death results in the condemnation of Satan as "the ruler of this world" (16:11). Thus, the "defense attorney" for Jesus' disciples acts as the "prosecuting attorney" against the world.

The adjoining Paraclete text (16:12-15) looks to the Spirit's function within the community. The Paraclete will extend the revelation brought by Jesus and supply what could not be understood during Jesus' life on earth (16:12). The Paraclete will guide the community in Jesus' way by stating Jesus' word afresh in new circumstances. The Spirit of Truth will not merely repeat Jesus' word nor set up a new word. Rather, the Paraclete will remain faithful to Jesus' word and apply it so as to glorify Jesus. The fidelity of the Paraclete is based in the unity that exists among Father, Son, and Spirit (16:15). Though one cannot speak of a fully developed theology of the Trinity in the New Testament, Johannine texts such as these clearly provided the biblical data for the decrees of the church councils (Nicea, Ephesus, Chalcedon) and made inevitable the early Christian efforts at defining the nature and relationships of the three persons. The Johannine point here is more modest: The departure of Jesus makes possible a fuller revelation and experience of God as Father, Son, and Spirit.

The second section (16:16-24) focuses on the disciples' reactions to what is going to happen to Jesus: their sorrow at his departure, and their joy at his return. The starting point is Jesus' mysterious saying: "A little while and you will no longer see me, and again a little while later and you will see me" (16:16). The monologue style that has prevailed since the beginning of chapter 15 is broken by the disciples' involved question about Jesus' meaning (16:17-19), which has the effect of highlighting both their lack of understanding and the importance of Jesus' reply.

The saying ("A little while. . . . ") refers first to Jesus' death and resurrection—his departure, which will be a sorrow to the disciples and a joy to the "world" (16:20). But the disciples' sorrow will turn to joy (see 16:20, 21, 22, 24), just as when a woman's pain in childbirth gives way to her joy over the birth of her child (16:21). Understanding Jesus' departure is easy enough. But his return to the disciples ("I will see you again," 16:22) is more problematic. When will he see his disciples again? Is it in the appearances immediately after his resurrection? Or is it in heavenly glory after their death? Or is it on the day of the Lord at the end of human history? Or is it on earth where Jesus' presence is prolonged by the Paraclete-Spirit? The saying about the disciples' having no more questions (16:23a) suggests the final day, whereas the idea of asking the Father in Jesus' name (16:23b; see 14:13-14) indicates the time of the Paraclete-Spirit. Attention to this problem should not distract from the marvelous idea that Jesus and his Father want us to pray "so that your joy may be complete" (16:24).

The farewell discourse ends in a dialogue between Jesus and his disciples (16:25-33). Jesus admits that he has been using figures of speech, perhaps a reference to the analogy of the woman giving birth (16:21) or perhaps an admission of the veiled or enigmatic speech about his departure and return. He promises plain speech in the "hour that is coming" (16:25). The same problem (when?) involved in 16:22 reappears here. On that day, Jesus will no longer need to serve as an intermediary between the Father and the disciples, since they will enjoy greater intimacy with the Father than ever before. John 16:28 summarizes the Gospel's teaching about Jesus: "I came from the Father and have come into the world. Now I am leaving the world and going back to the Father."

The clear summary of Johannine Christology in 16:28 leads the disciples to suppose that now Jesus is speaking plainly. They also attribute to Jesus omniscience ("you know everything") and even the ability to anticipate questions (16:30). The irony is that Jesus, in 16:31-32, uses their affirmation about Jesus' extraordinary knowledge as the occasion for him to prophecy their abandonment of him in the passion: "each of you will be scattered to his own home and you will leave me alone" (16:32). The other Gospels (Mark 14:27; Matt 26:31) connect this prophecy with the fulfillment of Zech 13:7: "I will strike the shepherd, and the sheep of the flock will be dispersed." Just when the Johannine disciples think that they finally understand Jesus' statements and who he is, Jesus uses his extraordinary power to show how little they do understand and how much they need the help and guidance of the Paraclete-Spirit. In 16:33 Jesus ends his farewell speeches in a positive manner by assuring the disciples of his ultimate victory ("I have conquered the world") and thus giving them a basis for peace in the present despite the opposition from the "world."

The Prayer of God's Son (17:1-26)

Since the sixteenth century, it has become customary to refer to John 17 as the "high priestly" prayer of Jesus, for in it Jesus makes intercession on behalf of his disciples and those who believe through them. There is clearly some justification for this title, though John never uses the "priestly" Christology found in the letter to the Hebrews. But the traditional characterization of the prayer may obscure the fact that John presents it as the prayer of God's Son who prays that his followers may share his intimate relationship with the Father.

Modern scholars sometimes call John 17 the "testament" of Jesus. A testament contains the last words of a departing hero. In it the hero looks over the past and into the future, and gives advice for those he leaves behind on how to behave. Testaments frequently conclude with the hero's prayer on behalf of his friends or children.

In his testament at the Last Supper, Jesus as Son of God prays for himself (17:1-5), for his disciples (17:6-19), and for those who come to believe through his disciples (17:20-26). There are some echoes of John 1:1-18 in the text, and no mention of the Paraclete-Spirit. Throughout (17:1, 5, 11, 21, 24, 25) Jesus addresses God as Father.

Jesus' prayer for himself (17:1-5) concerns the relation between his glory and his Father's glory. By looking up to heaven and addressing God as Father (17:1), Jesus creates the atmosphere of prayer. He announces that his "hour" (see 2:4; 7:30; 8:20; 12:23; 12:27; 13:1; 16:32) has finally arrived. He prays that the "hour" (passion, death, resurrection, exaltation) will be seen for what it truly is: a manifestation of God's glory. Just as in carrying out his work of revealing the Father, Jesus glorified God, now in the passion Jesus prays that he may again glorify God (17:1) and that God may glorify him (17:5). In the hour of Jesus, it will become apparent that Father and Son possess the same divine glory. The definition of "eternal life" (17:3) as knowledge of God and his messenger, Jesus, may be a later addition to the text, since it is clearly parenthetical and has the Son speak of himself as "Jesus Christ." So at the beginning of his hour, Jesus prays that what follows may be seen as the manifestation of God's glory. Thus, the reader of the Gospel is instructed to view the remainder of the Gospel not so much as a tragedy, but rather as an exaltation and a triumph.

The center of the testament of God's Son is his prayer for his disciples (17:6-19). Before making his prayer for them (17:9), Jesus gives a context that is more positive than the rest of the Gospel provides. The disciples are the ones to whom Jesus has revealed God and manifested God's glory; they have accepted Jesus' words and understood that he came from God (17:6-8). This picture contrasts sharply with the warning about the disciples' betrayal and abandonment of Jesus in 16:32. In his prayer, Jesus distinguishes his disciples from the "world" taken in its negative sense. Though the disciples are "in the world" (17:11, 13), they do not belong "to the world" (17:14,

16), that is, to the forces of evil arrayed against God and his Son. The disciples have been taken into the relationship existing between the Father and the Son. As he is about to depart, Jesus prays that they may continue in this relationship ("that they may be one just as we are," 17:11) and that God will keep them "from the evil one" (17:15; see Matt 6:13). But the Christians' posture is not purely defensive or self-protective. Rather, 17:18 emphasizes the theme of mission by completing the "sending" motif that runs through the Gospel: "As you sent me into the world, so I sent them into the world." Finally, Jesus prays that his disciples be swept up into the holiness and truth of God (17:17, 19). Oneness with God and his Son, mission, holiness, and truth—these are the gifts that God's Son asks from his Father on his disciples' behalf. The fragility of the disciples' situation is underscored not only by the references to opposition from the "world" (17:9, 14, 16), but also by the allusion to Judas as "the son of destruction" whose treachery and loss fulfilled the Scriptures (see 13:18).

Finally, in 17:20-26 the Son prays for those who will come to believe in Jesus through his disciples (17:20). The same points are made in 17:21 and 17:22-23, respectively: Jesus prays that all these may be one as he and the Father are one so that they may share this divine unity and they may come to believe that God sent the Son. Here, as 17:18, the "world" constitutes the object of the church's mission. The parallel structure in 17:21 and 17:22-23 is broken by the concluding clause of 17:23 ("and that you loved them even as you loved me"), which prepares for Jesus' wish at the very end of the prayer: "that the love with which you loved me may be in them and I in them" (17:26). Caught up in the mystery of love between Father and Son that existed before the creation of the world (17:24), the believers share in the divine glory, the divine unity, and the divine mission. The Son of God prays that his disciples and those who believe through him may enjoy the same relationship with the Father that he himself experiences. God's Son prays that we may be children of God also.

IV

The "Hour" of Jesus (18:1-21:25)

The Arrest of Jesus (18:1-27)

With the beginning of the passion account in chapter 18, John takes up the narrative that broke off at 14:31 ("Get up, let us go"). Throughout the passion narrative, John parallels the other Gospels. Yet the differences in details are so great and the perspectives so distinctive that it is hard to assume that John used the other Gospels directly.

John's passion narrative begins with the arrest of Jesus in the garden near Jerusalem (18:1-11). Then it tells how Jesus came to be questioned by Annas (18:12-14). Finally, it narrates Peter's denials of Jesus and Annas' questioning of Jesus (18:15-27). The two major episodes feature contrasts between the characters of Jesus and his disciples.

The arrest takes place in a garden east of Jerusalem (18:1); John does not name it Gethsemane or mention the Mount of Olives, though clearly the same place is meant in all four Gospels. Pilgrims coming to Jerusalem would frequently camp out in this area during Passover and other pilgrimage festivals. The original readers of the Gospel would have imagined the place to be crowded with pilgrims, not quiet and peaceful.

The actions of Judas the betrayer (18:2-3) and Peter (18:10-11) are contrasted with the conduct of Jesus (18:4-9). Judas knew where Jesus and his disciples were going, and so he organized a band of Roman soldiers as well as police under the direction of the chief priests and Pharisees (18:3). This mention of the Pharisees' involvement is unusual in the passion accounts, where the "chief priests and elders" are the leading Jewish figures. Some interpreters find in the reference to "lanterns and torches" the continuation of the "night" theme (see 13:30).

Judas' calculating treachery contrasts with Jesus' authoritative forthrightness (18:4-9). Jesus knows what is going to happen to him (18:4). When the arresting officers announce that they are looking for Jesus the Nazorean, Jesus identifies himself with the characteristic Johannine expression: "I AM," suggesting that even in arrest Jesus retains his connection with divinity (18:5, 6, 8). Whereas in the other Gospels Judas identifies Jesus with a kiss, here Jesus identifies himself. The reaction of the guards ("they turned away and fell to the ground," 18:6) indicates that they grasped the implications of Jesus' "I AM." Even in arrest, Jesus maintains his loving concern for his disciples (18:8-9) by arranging that they be let go (see 6:39; 10:11, 15, 28; 17:12).

Jesus' self-assurance and care for his disciples contrast with Peter's attempt to thwart the arrest of Jesus by violence (18:10-11). Only John identifies the swordsman as Peter and the slave as Malchus (see 18:26). Peter's violent resistance to the guards is the opposite of Jesus' peaceful submission to God's will symbolized by the image of the cup: "Shall I not drink the cup that the Father gave me?" (18:11; see Mark 10:38; Matt 20:22; 26:39; Luke 22:42).

How Jesus came to be questioned by Annas is explained in 18:12-14. The combination of Roman soldiers and Jewish guards brought Jesus to Annas, who had been high priest between A.D. 6 and 15 and retained influence through the high priesthood of his son-in-law, Caiaphas, between A.D. 18 and 36. There was no annual change of high priests, as 18:13 could be taken to suggest (see 11:51). Caiaphas, who was the high priest in "that (fateful) year," had unwittingly prophesied that Jesus' death would be on behalf of the whole people (18:14; see 11:49-50). The proceeding at the house of Annas (see 18:24) is a preliminary investigation or inquiry prior to the official trial before Pilate that begins in 18:28. There are no witnesses and no verdict. This proceeding is very different from the trial before the Sanhedrin described in Mark 14:55-65; Matt 26:59-68; Luke 22:66-71. According to John's chronology, the inquiry at Annas' house takes place the night before the beginning of Passover (the next evening).

The contrast in character between Peter (18:15-18, 25-27) and Jesus (18:19-24) is carried on in the next episode. The "sandwich" device in which Peter's denial of Jesus is interrupted by the trial of Jesus appears also in Mark 14:53-72 and Matt 26:57-75. Luke 22:54-71 presents them as separate episodes. The effect of the "sandwich" is to highlight the nobility of Jesus over against the cowardice of Peter.

John's story of Peter's denial of Jesus (18:15-18, 25-27) parallels the other Gospels in its basic outline. At the house of the high priest, Peter is identified three times as one of Jesus' disciples, and three times he denies any association with Jesus. In this way, he fulfills Jesus' prophecy in John 13:38: "The cock will not crow before you deny me three times." The most distinctively Johannine element is the appearance of "another disciple," one who was an acquaintance of the high priest and thus able to accompany Jesus into the courtyard and to get Peter in also (18:15-16). He is sometimes identified as the "beloved disciple" (see 13:23; 19:26; 20:2; 21:7) and serves as an eyewitness to the proceeding before Annas. The way in which Peter expresses his denial ("I am not") in 18:17, 25 serves as a foil to Jesus' previous confessions "I AM" (18:5, 6, 8). Finally, only John identifies the third inquirer (18:26) as a relative of Malchus whose ear Peter had cut off (see 18:10-11).

Whereas Peter cowers before his interrogators, Jesus stands up to the high priest Annas in 18:19-24. Behind Annas' questioning about Jesus' disciples and his doctrine may be the suspicion that Jesus is a false prophet (see Deuteronomy 13 and 18) who leads others astray by his teaching. Jesus refuses to cooperate in this process. He first demands that witnesses to his public teaching among the Jews be brought forward (18:20-21). He is confident that such witnesses will exonerate him. When struck by the temple guard (18:22), Jesus again proclaims his innocence: "If I have spoken wrongly, testify to the wrong; but if I have spoken rightly, why do you strike me?" (18:23). Though Annas sends Jesus off to Caiaphas

(18:24), we hear nothing about what happened at Caiaphas' house (18:28; compare Mark 14:55-65).

The Trial Before Pilate (18:28-19:16)

According to John, the only legal proceeding against Jesus was undertaken by the Roman governor, Pontius Pilate. After Herod Archelaus (son of Herod the Great) was deposed in A.D. 6, Judea was ruled directly by a Roman governor. The most famous of these Roman governors was Pontius Pilate who governed from A.D. 26 to 36. The ancient reports about Pilate present him as cruel and ruthless, quite different from the weak and vacillating character of the Gospels.

The Alexandrian Jewish writer Philo tells how Pontius Pilate brought into Jerusalem shields dedicated to the Roman emperor Tiberius—an act that was offensive to Jewish religious sensibilities. In *Legation to Gaius* Philo states that Pilate did this not so much to honor Tiberius as to annoy the multitude (299). He goes on to say that Pilate was "naturally inflexible, a blend of self-will and relentlessness" (301). According to Philo, Pilate only backed down on this matter "for he feared that if they actually sent an embassy (to the emperor Tiberius) they would also expose the rest of his conduct as governor by stating in full the briberies, the insults, the robberies, the outrages and wanton injuries, the executions without trial constantly repeated, the ceaseless and supremely grievous cruelty" (302).

John's portrayal of Jesus' trial before Pilate divides into seven scenes that alternate between outside and inside: A—the "Jews" seek Jesus' death (18:28-32); B—conversation between Pilate and Jesus (18:33-38a); C—Pilate finds Jesus innocent (18:38b-40); D—Jesus is hailed as "King of the Jews" (19:1-3); C1—Pilate finds Jesus innocent (19:4-8); B1—conversation between Pilate and Jesus (19:9-11); A1—the "Jews" obtain Jesus' death (19:12-16). At the heart of the story is the irony that Jesus, who is mocked as "King of the Jews," really is the King of the Jews for those who can see with the eyes of faith. Though the trial appears to be a defeat for Jesus, it is in fact a public manifestation and acknowledgment of his real identity.

The first scene (18:28-32) takes place outside. In the morning, the "Jews" (used in the negative sense to refer to Jesus' enemies) bring Jesus from Caiaphas, the Jewish high priest, to Pilate, the Roman governor. The scene takes place at the "praetorium," the residence of the Roman governor while he was in Jerusalem to oversee the pilgrimage and its crowds, lest an uprising break out. In order not to incur ritual impurity in a Gentile household before Passover, the "Jews" wish to remain outside and have Pilate come out to them. According to John, the beginning of Passover is still about twelve hours away. The conversation between the "Jews" and Pilate concerns why Jesus is being "handed over" (the term customarily used to describe Judas' betrayal). There is a dispute among historians whether the Jews at this time could execute other Jews. No matter how that dispute is resolved, what is important in John 18:28-32 is the suggestion as to what kind of criminal Jesus is alleged to be (a political rebel) and the appropriate punishment for such a crime (crucifixion administered by the Romans). It is possible to translate John 18:31: "We do not have the right to execute such one." The "lifting up" involved in crucifixion will fulfill Jesus' prophecies about his death (see 3:14; 8:28; 12:32-33), which to believers is an exaltation.

The second scene (18:33-38a) takes place inside the praetorium. Pilate asks Jesus whether he is the King of the Jews (18:33), which from Pilate's perspective would convey the idea of rebellion against Roman political control. Jesus, who is on trial and is being questioned, begins to question Pilate. The conversation makes clear that Jesus' kingdom is not an earthly, political kingdom (18:36). When Pilate persists, Jesus announces that his real mission has been "to testify to the truth" (18:37); that is, to reveal his heavenly Father. Pilate understands neither the nature of Jesus' kingship nor the truth.

The third scene (18:38b-40) occurs outside. Pilate declares to the "Jews" that he has found no guilt in Jesus (18:38; see 19:6). Again, there is a historical dispute regarding the "custom" of the Passover amnesty mentioned in 18:39. The real point comes, however, in the choice between Jesus and Barabbas. The name Barabbas can be analyzed into its parts "son" and "of the father/Abba." Barabbas is described as a "revolutionary" or "robber," probably a robber-bandit with political motives. So the choice before the "Jews" is between Jesus the genuine Son of the Father and King of the Jews, and Barabbas the revolutionary. They choose Barabbas.

The pivotal scene (19:1-3) takes place <u>inside</u>. John presents the scourging and mockery of Jesus prior to the final sentence and as part of Pilate's plan to release Jesus (see Mark 15:15-20; Matt 27:26-31). The mockery focuses on Jesus as "King of the Jews" and involves a thorny crown, a purple cloak, and a royal greeting. The irony is that, from the Christian perspective, Jesus really is the King of the Jews.

The fourth episode (19:4-8) occurs outside. Just as a newly crowned king is taken out to be acclaimed by his subjects, so Jesus the King of the Jews is taken out by Pilate, only to receive the decision "Crucify him, crucify him" (19:6). Pilate's strategy to elicit sympathy from the crowd backfires. When Pilate declares Jesus innocent (19:4) and tells the "Jews" to take care of Jesus on their own (19:6), they press him on the grounds that Jesus has committed blasphemy (see Lev 24:16) in referring to himself as the Son of God (see 5:18; 8:53; 10:36). The precise meaning of Pilate's words in 19:5 ("Behold, the man!") is not clear. They may emphasize the ridiculousness of the situation or seek to elicit pity. The <u>irony</u> is that Jesus is more than a mere man or even King of the Jews. He really is what the "Jews" say that he claims to be: the Son of God.

The sixth episode (19:9-11)—another conversation between Pilate and Jesus—occurs within the praetorium. Pilate's initial question to Jesus ("Where are you from?") on one level may reflect his plan to turn Jesus over to Herod Antipas (see Luke 23:6-7). But the thrust of the entire Gospel has been to show that Jesus is really from the Father. Whereas Pilate imagines that he has power over Jesus, in fact as God's Son, Jesus has power over Pilate (19:10-11a), since all political power comes ultimately from God (see Rom 13:1-7). But since Pilate does not understand all this, his sin is not as great as that of Judas who knew more and acted deliberately (19:11).

The final scene (19:12-16) takes place <u>outside</u>. The "Jews" put pressure on Pilate by suggesting that his willingness to

condemn Jesus will prove whether he deserves to be called
"friend of Caesar," probably an honorary title bestowed on
those who had done special services for the Roman emperor.
How the "Jews" obtain a death sentence for Jesus is told in
great detail, giving the time (about noon, on the day leading
up to Passover) and the place ("Stone Pavement") and allowing
us to envision the scene of Pilate seated at the official judge's
bench (19:13-14). The dialogue between Pilate and the "Jews'
elicits their rejection of Jesus as king and their acceptance of
the Roman emperor—a shocking irony in view of longstanding
Jewish opposition to foreign domination and what happened
in A.D. 70 when the Romans destroyed Jerusalem and its
temple. With these admissions, Pilate hands Jesus over to the
chief priests (19:16), though it is clear that the Romans eventually carry out the execution (19:19, 23).

ONY   The use of irony, which has been prominent throughout the
Gospel, reaches its climax in the trial before Pilate. Both writer
and reader know that Jesus is King of the Jews and Son of
God. Pilate and the "Jews", by their words and actions, tell the
truth about Jesus even though they seem not to know it or
believe it. The challenge to the reader today is to face the
question: What do you see in Jesus' trial? Do you see only the
external appearances that Pilate and the "Jews" saw? Or do
you see what was really happening—a step in the exaltation of
God's Son?

The Death of Jesus (19:17-42)

The account of Jesus' death follows a pattern similar to the
narrative of the trial before Pilate, though the symmetry is not
quite so neat and the outside-inside alternation of scenes is
absent. At the center of the account is the scene of Jesus
speaking from the cross to his mother and the beloved disciple
(19:25-27). On the one side, the central scene is introduced by
three scenes: A—crucifixion (19:17-18); B—the Jews' request
(19:19-22); C—Scripture fulfilled (19:23-24). On the other side,
it is followed by three scenes: C1—Scripture fulfilled (19:28-30);
B1—the Jews' request (19:31-37); A1—burial (19:38-42).

The act of crucifixion (19:17-18) is described very briefly. As master of his own destiny, Jesus carries his own cross; there is no mention of Simon of Cyrene (Mark 15:21; Matt 27:32; Luke 23:26). The crucifixion takes place outside the ancient wall of Jerusalem at the "Place of the Skull" (*Calvaria* in Latin, Golgotha in Aramaic), so called because it was a hill where criminals were executed. Jesus is crucified along with two others (see Isa 53:12, "he was counted among the wicked"). Like the other Evangelists, John does not dwell upon the physical sufferings (which were great) involved in crucifixion. They were more interested in the significance of Jesus' death than in its details.

The first request made by the "Jews" (19:19-22) concerns the wording of the charge against Jesus. Pilate writes "Jesus the Nazorean, the King of the Jews" (19:19), reflecting his perception of Jesus as a political rebel against the empire. When the "Jews" object that this was only Jesus' claim and not theirs, Pilate lets the wording stand, presumably to insult and humiliate the "Jews" by suggesting that this is what a Jewish king looks like. His intended irony is overtaken by the irony that the Christian reader finds here: The Roman official proclaims to the world (in three languages!) that Jesus is the King of the Jews.

In 19:23-24 Scripture is fulfilled with reference to Psalm 22:19. First the soldiers divide Jesus' garments among themselves (19:23a=Ps 22:19a). Then, they cast lots for his tunic (19:23b-24a=Ps 22:19b). Psalm 22 is the classic biblical statement of the righteous sufferer. When early Christians talked about Jesus' suffering and death, they often went to Psalm 22 for their language and theology (see Mark 15:34). Some interpreters find in the seamless tunic of Jesus a symbol for the unity of the church constituted by his death on the cross. Others see in it a reminder of the dress of the Jewish high priest (Exodus 28).

The scene at the foot of the cross (19:25-27) features the mother of Jesus and the "beloved disciple." Whether we are to imagine three or four women depends on whether "and his mother's sister, Mary the wife of Clopas" (19:25) refers to one or two persons. In the other Gospels, the women look on from a distance (Mark 15:40). The final command given by Jesus (19:26-27) is the dramatic climax of the Johannine passion narrative. Yet it is ambiguous. Is the beloved disciple to take Jesus' mother "into his own home" or as his own mother in faith? Moreover, if we ascribe to the episode a symbolic value, what does it symbolize? Is Mary Israel or the church or the mother of Christians? There need not be only one answer to these questions, given the nature of symbols.

In 19:28-30 Scripture is fulfilled with Jesus' cry: "I thirst," probably an allusion to Ps 22:16 ("My throat is dried up like baked clay, my tongue cleaves to my jaws") and to Ps 69:22 ("in my thirst they gave me vinegar to drink"). That a sprig of hyssop (which has no stalk) could not support a sponge soaked with wine (to ease the pain) causes interpreters to emend the text ("switch, javelin") or to find some symbolic reference to Jesus as the Passover lamb (Exod 12:22). According to John's chronology, Jesus died when the Passover lambs were being sacrificed in the Jerusalem temple. Jesus' last word in 19:30 ("It is finished") carries also the nuances of fulfillment (of God's will expressed in the Scriptures) and perfection (the death of God's Son "who takes away the sin of the world," 1:29). The phrase "he handed over the spirit" (19:30) can be taken to describe Jesus' dying (giving up his last breath) and/or his bestowal of the Holy Spirit at the moment of his death (see 7:39; 20:22).

The second request made by the "Jews" (19:31-37) is that the legs of the crucified ones (including Jesus) be broken (to prevent the person from remaining erect and continuing to breathe) before the celebration of Passover began. The description of what happens is designed to prove that Jesus was really dead and that the details surrounding his death fulfilled the Scriptures. That Jesus really died is proved first by the soldiers' refusal to break his legs (19:33), then by the flow of blood and water from his side (19:34), and finally, by the testimony of an eyewitness (19:35, presumably the "beloved disciple"). These proofs rule out the idea that Jesus merely went into shock and later revived. In Christian piety, the blood and water from Jesus' side have often been associated with the sacraments of the Eucharist and baptism. The soldiers' refusal to break Jesus' legs fulfills Exod 12:46 ("not a bone of it [the Passover Lamb] will be broken"). The piercing of Jesus' side fulfills Zech 12:10 ("They will look upon him whom they have pierced").

The burial of Jesus (19:38-42) is carried out by Joseph of Arimathea and Nicodemus. Only John mentions that Joseph was a secret disciple "for fear of the Jews" and that Nicodemus (see 3:1-2; 7:50) took part in Jesus' burial. Their actions in anointing Jesus' body (19:39), binding it with burial cloths (19:40), and placing it in a tomb near the site of Jesus' death (19:41) signify their failure to understand what is about to happen to the one who proclaimed himself to be "the resurrection and the life" (11:25).

While John does not ignore the physical sufferings of Jesus, he does try to underline the significance of Jesus' death in various ways: He fulfills God's will expressed in the Scriptures; he really is the King of the Jews; the Lamb of God is executed when the Passover lambs are being slaughtered in the Jerusalem temple.

Easter Faith (20:1-31)

Perhaps the most distinctive belief among the early Christians was their claim that Jesus was raised from dead at Easter. From their perspective of Easter faith, the early Christians looked back on Jesus' life and grew in their understanding and appreciation of his person, work, and teaching. John 20 traces the origin and development of Easter faith. It consists of four stories: Peter and the beloved disciple at the empty tomb (20:1-10), Jesus' appearance to Mary Magdalene (20:11-18), his appearance to the disciples (20:19-25), and his appearance to Thomas (20:26-29). In these narratives, the followers of Jesus pass from doubt to faith and from confusion to confession. The epilogue to the Gospel (20:30-31) suggests how those who do not experience what the first disciples did can come to believe in Jesus.

All four Gospels tell the story of the empty tomb on Easter Sunday morning (John 20:1-10; Mark 16:1-8; Matt 28:1-10; Luke 24:1-12). The question that the story raises is, How did the tomb come to be empty? Whereas the other Evangelists explain through a young man/angel that Jesus had been raised from the dead, John makes the fact of Jesus' resurrection to be the deduction drawn by the beloved disciple. On Easter Sunday morning, Mary Magdalene, who had witnessed Jesus' death (19:25), found that the stone covering the mouth of Jesus' burial cave had been rolled away (20:1). Her deduction was that Jesus' corpse had been stolen from the tomb (20:2). Since grave-robbing was common then, it was a logical deduction. The next visitors to the tomb are Peter and the beloved disciple (20:3; Luke 24:12). They confirm that Jesus' tomb was empty. But the beloved disciple draws a different conclusion. Whereas Peter "saw the burial cloths there" (20:6), the beloved disciple "saw and believed" (20:8). The key to the beloved disciple's deduction was the positioning of Jesus' burial garments: "the burial cloths there, and the cloth that had covered his head, not with the burial cloths but rolled up in a separate place" (20:6-7). The beloved disciple recognized the disposition of Jesus' burial garments as a sign that Jesus had been raised from the dead. Perhaps the similarities with the Lazarus episode (11:44) led him so to believe. This deduction did not come easily. Jews of Jesus' time who believed in resurrection expected it to be a communal event at the end of human history. Belief in the resurrection of an individual before the end of history was without precedent. And the disciples still did not (or, had not up to this point) understood about the Old Testament as a witness to Jesus' resurrection (20:9; see 1 Cor 15:4; Luke 24:25-27, 44-47).

Resurrection means that the whole person—body and soul—comes to life again. Jews in Jesus' time expected the resurrection to occur at the Last Judgment, as the end of human history. They also expected that the resurrection would encompass many (or all) people. Daniel 12:1-3 provides such a picture of the resurrection of the dead:

> "At that time there shall arise
>   Michael, the great prince,
>   guardian of your people;
> It shall be a time unsurpassed in distress
>   since nations began until that time.

At that time your people shall escape,
    everyone who is found written in the book.
Many of those who sleep
    in the dust of the earth shall awake:
Some shall live forever,
    others shall be an everlasting horror and
      disgrace.
But the wise shall shine brightly
    like the splendor of the firmament.
And those who lead the many to justice
    shall be like the stars forever.

The risen Jesus' appearance to Mary Magdalene (20:11-18) is the next step in the development of Easter faith. This story links together the empty tomb and the appearances. Mary, who had discovered the stone removed from Jesus' tomb (20:1), now finds the tomb empty and repeats her deduction that Jesus' body had been stolen (20:13). Her mind is changed by an appearance of the risen Lord (20:14-18). At first, she understands neither the empty tomb nor the identity of Jesus. Only when Jesus calls her by name (20:16), does Mary recognize him and believe that she had seen the Lord (20:18). John makes Mary Magdalene the special witness to Jesus' resurrection by mentioning only her at the tomb (20:1; see Mark 16:1) and by making her the sole recipient of the first appearance (20:14-18; see Matt 28:9-10). The precise meaning of Jesus' command in 20:17 ("Stop holding on to me") has eluded interpreters. Does it mean simply that, instead of trying to hold on to Jesus, Mary should go about her task of preparing the disciples for the coming of the Spirit? Or does Jesus' ascension take place between this and the next episode? What does the command imply about the "body" of the risen Lord?

The first appearance to the disciples as a group (20:19-25) takes place on Easter Sunday evening. Even though the doors are locked "for fear of the Jews," Jesus enters mysteriously and greets the disciples in the usual way: "Peace be with you." There is an effort to stress both the extraordinary character of the risen Jesus (his sudden appearance) and his continuity with the crucified Jesus ("he showed them his hands and his side," 20:20). The Easter appearance is John's equivalent of Pentecost. The risen Jesus proposes the Father's sending of the Son as the model and basis for his sending of the disciples (20:21). He equips them for mission with the gift of the Holy Spirit (20:22) and grants them power over sin (20:23; see Matt 16:19; 18:18). In this context, Jesus' use of the greeting "Peace" takes on more than its customary meaning. Thomas wants the same experience as the other disciples had (20:24-25). He wants to touch the body of the risen Jesus to satisfy himself that it is the same Jesus.

The second appearance to the disciples as a group (20:24-29) takes place the following Sunday and includes Thomas. It follows the same outline: Jesus enters mysteriously, greets the disciples, and proves his continuity with the crucified Jesus. When Thomas sees the risen Lord, all his doubts dissolve, and he makes the most perfect profession of faith in the Gospel ("My Lord and my God," 20:28). As the Gospel began by affirming that "the Word was God" (1:1), so it ends with the confession of Jesus as Lord and God. In 20:29 Jesus compares the faith shown by Thomas and the other disciples (they saw and believed) with the faith of those who do not see and yet believe. The object of faith is the same: Jesus has been raised from the dead. The mode of belief differs: sight and belief versus simple belief.

Belief without sight is demanded from those who read John's Gospel. And so the Evangelist explains his purpose in writing the Gospel: "that you may believe that Jesus is the Messiah, the Son of God, and that through this belief you may have life in his name" (20:31). There is an old dispute about the meaning of the verb "that you may believe": Does it mean "come to believe" (suggesting that the Gospel was written for non-Christians), or "continue to believe" (suggesting that the intention was to deepen the faith of those who already believed)? At any rate, the epilogue reminds us of the two central themes of the Gospel: the identity of Jesus, and his gift of eternal life to those who believe in him.

Appendix: Peter and the Beloved Disciple (21:1-25)

It has become customary to refer to chapter 21 as an appendix, or addition, to John's Gospel. This designation is based on the facts that John 20:30-31 seems to be the conclusion of the entire Gospel and that chapter 21 is only loosely related to the first twenty chapters. Its basic function is to tie up some loose ends: the fates of Peter and the beloved disciple, the care of the flock after Jesus' departure, and the relationship of the Evangelist to the beloved disciple. It is introduced by an appearance story (21:1-14) that features Peter and the beloved disciple.

The appearance of the risen Lord (21:1-14) takes place at the Sea of Tiberias, another name for the Sea of Galilee, taken from the city of Tiberias on its western shore. Whereas the appearances in chapter 20 take place in Jerusalem (see also Luke 24), the appearance in chapter 21 occurs in Galilee (see also Matthew 28). Peter and the other disciples have returned to their jobs as fishermen and show no special effect from the Jerusalem appearances (21:2-3). The story of their unsuccessful effort at fishing and its resolution by Jesus is similar to the call of the disciples according to Luke 5:1-11. There is a long-standing debate whether Luke 5:1-11 was originally a resurrection-appearance story tailored to fit Jesus' earthly ministry, or John 21:1-14 was a call narrative that has been adapted as an appearance account. In the present Johannine context at least, the disciples succeed by following the word of Jesus (21:6). As in the empty tomb story (20:8), the beloved disciple recognizes the reality behind the appearances: "It is the Lord!" (21:7). As the story proceeds, Peter emerges as the most prominent among the disciples. He jumps into the sea (21:7; see Matt 14:22-25) and later brings the catch of fish to Jesus (21:11). The precise number of fish at 153 has fascinated interpreters for centuries; it has been explained in terms of historical fact, mathematical symbolism (the sum of all numbers from one to seventeen), biblical allusions (Ezek 47:10), and gematria (using numbers to stand for letters). Most interpreters find in the number and the untorn net (21:11) a reference to the church and its mission. By sharing a meal of bread and fish with his disciples by the Sea of Galilee, the risen Lord does what the earthly Jesus did in feeding the crowd of 5,000 (6:1-14). Jesus' ability to eat a meal indicates that, in his risen state, he is more than a ghost or a vision. Moreover, there may also be a "eucharistic" dimension to the risen Lord sharing a meal with his disciples (see Luke 24:30, 42). This appearance story is counted as the third in the series to the disciples (21:14); the appearance to Mary Magdalene as an individual is not counted. Though perhaps not part of John's Gospel at one point, John 21:1-14 fits well with the rest of the Gospel: the setting in Galilee, the Lord's presence, the revelation of Jesus' identity, the beloved disciple and Peter, and the call to mission.

The remainder of the appendix concerns Peter (21:15-19) and the beloved disciple (21:20-25). The dialogue between the risen Jesus and Peter serves to rehabilitate Peter and designate him as the chief "pastor" of the flock (the church). Just as in John 18:15-18, 25-27 Peter denied Jesus three times, so in John 21:15-17 Peter affirms his love for Jesus three times. The dialogue features synonyms for love, feed, know, and sheep. With the proverb about the independence of youth and the constraints of old age (21:18), Jesus alludes to the martyrdom of Peter, understood in early Christian tradition as crucifixion at Rome. Jesus' summons "Follow me" (21:19) suggests that following Jesus involves sharing his death.

After Peter emerges as pastor and martyr, John 21 seeks to clear up two mysteries associated with the beloved disciple. The first mystery concerns the relation between his death and the Lord's second coming as expressed in an otherwise unknown saying of Jesus: "What if I want him to remain until I come?" (21:22, 23). The beloved disciple had probably died recently. But Jesus had not come again. The point of the passage is to correct the assumption that the beloved disciple would not die before Jesus' second coming. The thrust of the "correction" (21:23) is to leave that decision to the risen Lord; it is no one else's business but his. The saying is ambiguous.

The second mystery (21:24-25) concerns the relation of the beloved disciple to the writing of the Fourth Gospel. This "second conclusion" to the Gospel affirms that the beloved disciple has provided written testimony. But the assertion "we know that his testimony is true" suggests some distance between him and the present writer. The idea that the Gospel is only a selection of things that Jesus did (21:25) repeats what was said in 20:30.

For Reference and Further Study

Major Commentaries

C. K. Barrett. *The Gospel According to St. John. An Introduction with Commentary and Notes on the Greek Text.* 2nd ed. Philadelphia: Westminster, 1978.

G. R. Beasley-Murray. *John.* Waco, TX: Word, 1987.

R. E. Brown. *The Gospel According to John. Introduction, Translation, and Notes.* 2 vols. New York: Doubleday, 1966, 1970.

F. F. Bruce. *The Gospel of John. Introduction, Exposition and Notes.* Grand Rapids: Eerdmans, 1983.

R. Bultmann. *The Gospel of John. A Commentary.* Philadelphia: Westminster, 1971.

E. Haenchen. *John. A Commentary on the Gospel of John.* 2 vols. Philadelphia: Fortress, 1984.

B. Lindars. *The Gospel of John.* Greenwood, SC: Attic Press, 1972.

J. McPolin. *John.* Rev. ed. Wilmington: Glazier, 1982.

R. Schnackenburg. *The Gospel According to St. John.* 3 vols. New York: Crossroad, 1968/80, 1979/81, 1982.

Important Books

J. Ashton (ed.). *The Interpretation of John.* Philadelphia: Fortress, 1986.

R. E. Brown. *The Community of the Beloved Disciple.* New York—Ramsey, NJ—Toronto: Paulist, 1979.

O. Cullmann. *The Johannine Circle.* Philadelphia: Fortress, 1976.

R. A. Culpepper. *Anatomy of the Fourth Gospel: A Study in Literary Design*. Philadelphia: Fortress, 1983.

C. H. Dodd. *The Interpretation of the Fourth Gospel*. New York—London: Cambridge University Press, 1953.

_____. *Historical Tradition in the Fourth Gospel*. New York—London: Cambridge University Press, 1963.

P. D. Duke. *Irony in the Fourth Gospel*. Atlanta: John Knox, 1985.

R. T. Fortna. *The Fourth Gospel and Its Predecessor: From Narrative Source to Present Gospel*. Philadelphia: Fortress, 1988.

F. Manns. *John and Jamnia: How the Break Occurred Between Jews and Christians c. 80-100 A.D.* Jerusalem: Franciscan Printing Press, 1988.

J. L. Martyn. *History and Theology in the Fourth Gospel*. 2nd rev. ed. Nashville: Abingdon, 1979.

J. H. Neyrey. *An Ideology of Revolt. John's Christology in Social-Science Perspective*. Philadelphia: Fortress, 1988.

M. J. Taylor (ed.). *A Companion to John. Readings in Johannine Theology (John's Gospel and Epistles)*. New York: Alba House, 1977.

U. C. von Wahlde. *The Earliest Version of John's Gospel. Recovering the Gospel of Signs*. Wilmington: Glazier, 1989.

Spirituality

L. W. Countryman. *The Mystical Way in the Fourth Gospel. Crossing Over into God*. Philadelphia: Fortress, 1987.

L. Doohan. *John: Gospel for a new age*. Santa Fe, NM: Bear & Co., 1988.

G. R. O'Day. *The Word Disclosed. John's Story and Narrative Preaching*. St. Louis, MO: CBP Press, 1987.

D. M. Stanley. *"I Encountered God!" The Spiritual Exercises with the Gospel of John.* St. Louis, MO: Institute of Jesuit Sources, 1986.

J. Wijngaards. *The Gospel of John and His Letters.* Wilmington: Glazier, 1986.

Bibliographies

E. Malatesta. *St. John's Gospel 1920-1965. A Cumulative and Classified Bibliography of Books and Periodical Literature on the Fourth Gospel.* Rome: Pontifical Biblical Institute, 1967.

G. Van Belle. *Johannine Bibliography 1966-1985. A Cumulative Bibliography on the Fourth Gospel.* Leuven: Leuven University Press—Peeters, 1988. (Ongoing bibliography appears in *New Testament Abstracts*.)

Appendix

John's Gospel
in the Lectionary

In the lectionary used by the Roman Catholic and other Christian churches there is a three-year cycle of Gospel readings that features a different Synoptic Gospel each year: Matthew (series A 1990, 1993, 1996, 1999, etc.); Mark (series B 1991, 1994, 1997, 2000, etc.) and Luke (series C 1992, 1995, 1998, 2001, etc.). Selections from John's Gospel are interspersed in each of the three cycles. Moreover, important liturgical feasts are marked by readings from John's Gospel. For a proposal about a separate series (year D) based on John's Gospel, see D. L. Conrad, "Why Not Also a Series on John?" *Currents in Theology and Mission* 15 (1988) 349-55. The following lists show where texts from the Fourth Gospel appear in the present lectionary.

A. By Liturgical Seasons

1. *Sundays in Lent*
   Year A: 3rd to 5th, John 4:5-42; 9:1-41; 11:1-45.
   Year B: 3rd to 5th, John 2:13-25 or 4:5-42; 3:14-21 or 9:1-41; 11:1-45 or 12:20-33.
   Year C: 3rd to 5th, John 4:5-42; 9:1-41; 8:1-11 or 11:1-45.

2. *Sundays in the Easter Season*
   Year A: 2nd, 4th to 7th, John 20:19-31; 10:1-10; 14:1-12; 14:15-21; 17:1-11.

Year B: 2nd to 7th, John 20:19-31; 21:1-19; 10:11-18;
15:1-8; 15:9-17; 17:11-19.

Year C: 2nd to 7th, John 20:19-31; 21:1-19; 10:27-30;
13:31-33; 14:23-29; 17:20-26.

3. *Sundays in Ordinary Time*
Year A: 2nd, John 1:29-34.
Year B: 2nd, John 1:35-42; 17th to 21st, John 6:1-15;
6:24-35; 6:41-51; 6:51-58; 6:60-69.
Year C: 2nd, John 2:1-12.

4. *Major Feasts*
Years A, B, C: Christmas, John 1:1-18; Holy Thursday,
13:1-15; Good Friday, 18:1-19:42; Easter, 20:1-9; Vigil
of Pentecost, 7:37-39; Pentecost, 20:19-23.

5. *Other Feasts*
Year A: Trinity Sunday, John 3:16-18; Corpus Christi,
6:51-58.
Year B: 3rd Sunday of Advent, John 1:6-8, 19-28;
Sacred Heart, 19:31-37; Christ the King, 18:33-37.
Year C: Trinity Sunday, John 16:12-15.

6. *Weekdays in Lent*
Week 3: John 4:5-42 (optional).
Week 4: M to Th, John 4:43-5:47; F to S, 7:1-53; 9:1-41
(optional).
Week 5: M to Th, John 8:1-59; F, 10:31-42; S, 11:45-56;
11:1-45 (optional).
Week 6: M, John 12:1-11; T, 13:21-33, 36-38.

7. *Weekdays in the Easter Season*
Week 1: T, 20:11-18; F, 21:1-14.
Week 2: M to Th, 3:1-36; F to S, 6:1-21.
Week 3: M to F, 6:22-69.
Week 4: M to T, 10:1-30; W, 12:44-50; Th, 13:16-20; F
to S, 14:1-14.
Week 5: M to S, 14:21-15:21.
Week 6: M to S, 15:26-16:28.
Week 7: M to Th, 16:29-17:26; F to S, 20:15-25.

8. *Weekdays Around Christmas*
Friday, Third Week of Advent, John 5:33-36.

December 31 to January 7, John 1:1-2:12.
January 12, John 3:22-30.

B. Johannine Texts for Sundays and Major Feasts

The annotations beside the texts (e.g., A 2 Lent) refer to the Year (A, B, C), the Sunday number (2, 3, 4, etc.), and the Liturgical Season (Lent, Easter, Ordinary Time).

1:1-18	ABC Christmas
1:6-8, 19-28	B 3 Advent
1:29-34	A 2 Ord.
1:35-42	B 2 Ord.
2:1-12	C 2 Ord.
2:13-25	B 3 Lent
3:14-21	B 4 Lent
3:16-18	A Trinity Sunday
4:5-42	ABC 3 Lent
6:1-15	B 17 Ord.
6:24-35	B 18 Ord.
6:41-51	B 19 Ord.
6:51-58	B 20 Ord., A Corpus Christi
6:60-69	B 21 Ord.
7:37-39	ABC Vigil of Pentecost
8:1-11	C 5 Lent
9:1-41	ABC 4 Lent
10:1-10	A 4 Easter
10:11-18	B 4 Easter
10:27-30	C 4 Easter
11:1-45	ABC 5 Lent
12:20-33	B 5 Lent
12:12-16	B Palm Sunday
13:1-15	ABC Holy Thursday
13:31-33	C 5 Easter
14:1-12	A 5 Easter
14:15-21	A 6 Easter
14:23-29	C 6 Easter
15:1-8	B 5 Easter

15:9-17	B 6 Easter
16:12-15	C Trinity Sunday
17:1-11	A 7 Easter
17:11-19	B 7 Easter
17:20-26	C 7 Easter
18:1-19:42	ABC Good Friday
18:33-37	B Christ the King
19:31-37	B Sacred Heart
20:1-9	ABC Easter
20:19-23	ABC Pentecost
20:19-31	ABC 2 Easter
21:1-19	BC 3 Easter